Praise for *They*

"In this powerful series of rep_____ ___ ___ ___ _ague's international courtroom, Slavenka Drakulić confronts the Yugoslav War's grand villains and banal perpetrators, as she fearlessly contemplates both the individual character of evil and the tragic, chillingly impersonal mechanisms of war. Writing with her hallmark blend of forthrightness, open-eyed irony, and psychological discernment, Drakulić gives us disturbingly intimate vignettes of war criminals who might have been her own (and our) neighbors, even as she illuminates one of our time's most daunting and urgent questions: How ordinary men and women turn, and are turned into, genocidal killers. An important and a necessary book."   —Eva Hoffman

"How could people who once lived together in peace, and who now have returned to tolerance in prison, have committed war crimes and mass atrocities against each other? This is the question Slavenka Drakulić dares to ask in *They Would Never Hurt a Fly*. With the curiosity of a journalist and the empathy of a novelist, she allows us to see that ordinary people—when fed a belief in hierarchy within families and nationalism in our history books—are capable of the greatest evil: an absence of empathy. This lesson from the former Yugoslavia is as current as today's headlines from Iraq and the Sudan."
                                                                —Gloria Steinem

"Lucidly written . . . a devastating book. . . . [Drakulić's] direct, personal style does justice to the weight and grimness of these stories."
                                                        —*The Guardian* (London)

"[A] highly readable, persuasive book . . . In spite of its disturbing content, Drakulić's measured tone, her conviction that the only way forward for humanity is to face up to our lack of humanity carries the reader through."   —*Irish Examiner*

"This is one of the most harrowing books you will read this year—but read it you must."   —*Evening Herald* (UK)

PENGUIN BOOKS

THEY WOULD NEVER HURT A FLY

Slavenka Drakulić was born in Croatia in 1949. Her nonfiction books include *How We Survived Communism and Even Laughed*, *The Balkan Express: Fragments from the Other Side of the War*, and *Café Europa: Life After Communism* (Penguin). Drakulić is also the author of the novels *Holograms of Fear*, which was a bestseller in Yugoslavia and was short-listed for the Best Foreign Book Award by *The Independent* (UK), *Marble Skin*, *The Taste of a Man* (Penguin), and *S.* (Penguin). A freelance journalist who contributes to *The New York Times*, *The Nation*, *The New Republic*, *Frankfurter Allgemeine Zeitung* (Germany), *Dagens Nyheter* (Sweden), and *La Stampa* (Italy), as well as other magazines and newspapers, she now divides her time among Sweden, Austria, and Croatia.

They Would Never Hurt a Fly

War Criminals on Trial in The Hague

Slavenka Drakulić

PENGUIN BOOKS

PENGUIN BOOKS

Published by the Penguin Group
Penguin Group (USA) Inc., 375 Hudson Street, New York, New York 10014, U.S.A.
Penguin Group (Canada), 10 Alcorn Avenue, Toronto, Ontario,
    Canada M4V 3B2 (a division of Pearson Penguin Canada Inc.)
Penguin Books Ltd, 80 Strand, London WC2R 0RL, England
Penguin Ireland, 25 St Stephen's Green, Dublin 2, Ireland (a division of Penguin Books Ltd)
Penguin Group (Australia), 250 Camberwell Road, Camberwell,
    Victoria 3124, Australia (a division of Pearson Australia Group Pty Ltd)
Penguin Books India Pvt Ltd, 11 Community Centre, Panchsheel Park, New Delhi - 110 017, India
Penguin Group (NZ), cnr Airborne and Rosedale Roads, Albany,
    Auckland 1310, New Zealand (a division of Pearson New Zealand Ltd)
Penguin Books (South Africa) (Pty) Ltd, 24 Sturdee Avenue, Rosebank,
    Johannesburg 2196, South Africa

Penguin Books Ltd, Registered Offices:
80 Strand, London WC2R 0RL, England

First published in the United States of America by Viking Penguin,
a member of Penguin Group (USA) Inc. 2004
Published in Penguin Books 2005

10 9 8 7 6 5 4 3 2 1

Published as *Oni ne bi ni mrava zgazili* by Biblioteka Feral Tribute (Split, 2003) in a translation from the
original English to Croatian by Rujana Jeger.

THE LIBRARY OF CONGRESS HAS CATALOGED THE HARDCOVER EDITION AS FOLLOWS:
Drakulić, Slavenka, 1949–
They would never hurt a fly: war criminals on trial in The Hague/Slavenka Drakulić
p. cm.
ISBN 0-670-03332-4 (hc.)
ISBN 0 14 30.3542 8 (pbk.)
1. Yugoslav War, 1991–1995—Atrocities. 2. War criminals—Serbia and Montengero—
Serbia—Psychology. 3. Political culture—Serbia and Montenegro—Serbia.
4. War criminals—Croatia—Psychology. 5. Political culture—Croatia. 6. International Tribunal
for the Prosecution of Persons Responsible for Serious Violations of International Humanitarian Law
Committed in the Territory of the Former Yugoslavia since 1991. 7. Yugoslav War Crime Trials,
Hague, Netherlands. 1994– 8. Nationalism—Former Yugoslav republics.
I. Title: War criminals on trial in The Hague. II. Title
DR1313.7 A85D7 2004
949.703—dc22   2003065768

Printed in the United States of America
Designed by Carla Bolte • Set in Spectrum • Map drawn by James Sinclair

He has driven the dichotomy of private and public functions, of family and occupation, so far that he can no longer find in his own person any connection between the two. When his occupation forces him to murder people he does not regard himself as a murderer because he has not done it out of inclination but in his professional capacity. Out of sheer passion he would never do harm to a fly.

—Hannah Arendt, *Essays in Understanding, 1930–1954*

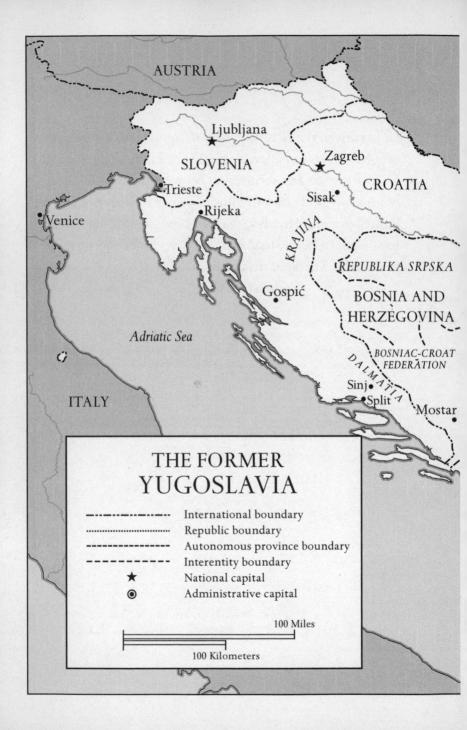

AUSTRIA

Ljubljana ★

SLOVENIA

Trieste

Venice

Rijeka

Zagreb ★

Sisak •

CROATIA

KRAJINA

REPUBLIKA SRPSKA

Gospić •

BOSNIA AND
HERZEGOVINA

Adriatic Sea

DALMATIA

BOSNIAC-CROAT
FEDERATION

Sinj •

Split •

Mostar •

ITALY

THE FORMER
YUGOSLAVIA

— ·· — ·· —   International boundary
· · · · · · · · ·   Republic boundary
— — — — —   Autonomous province boundary
— — — — —   Interentity boundary
★   National capital
◉   Administrative capital

100 Miles

100 Kilometers

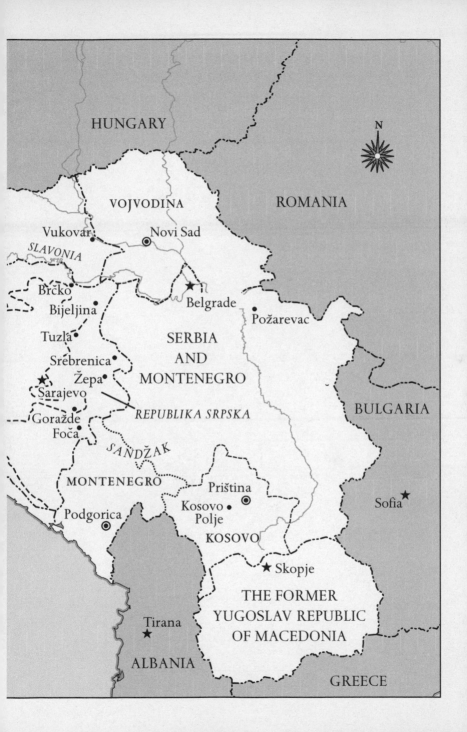

Contents

They Would Never Hurt a Fly

Introduction: Not a Fairy Tale

O NCE UPON a time, in a faraway part of Europe, behind
seven mountains and seven rivers, there was a beautiful country called Yugoslavia. Its people belonged to six
different nations, and they were of three different religions
and spoke three different languages. They were Croats, Serbs,
Slovenes, Macedonians, Montenegrins, and Muslims yet
they all worked together, went to school together, married
each other, and lived in relative harmony for forty-five years.

But because it is not a fairy tale, the story of this beautiful
country has no happy ending. Yugoslavia fell apart in a terrible and bloody war, a war that claimed some two hundred
thousand lives—mostly in Bosnia—displaced two million
people, and produced several new states: Slovenia, Bosnia,
Croatia, Serbia, and Macedonia. Albanians and Montenegrins are still struggling for their independence.

This all happened in the middle of Europe not so long
ago, between 1991 and 1995. The whole world was surprised
by this war. We, the citizens of Yugoslavia, were even more
surprised. When I think about it, I am still angry with myself.
Is it possible that the war crept into our lives slowly, stealth-

ily, like a thief? Why didn't we see it coming? Why didn't we do something to prevent it? Why were we so arrogant that we thought it could not happen to us? Were we really prisoners of a fairy tale?

My generation in Europe grew up believing that after World War II, war of that kind could not happen again. Nuclear war between two superpowers was a possibility, not a local one fought with conventional arms. Another argument against the likelihood of a new war was that in World War II in Yugoslavia, hundreds of thousands of people perished on all sides. The witnesses were still alive, the wounds were still open. And finally, we knew that Yugoslavia had no enemies. We lived peacefully with our neighbors: with Italians, Austrians, Hungarians, Romanians, Bulgarians, and Albanians.

But one day we discovered that it is not necessary to have an outside enemy to start a war. The enemy could be inside—and indeed it was. It was bad enough digging up the past—the past that we tend to forget, that during the war Yugoslavia was occupied or controlled by Nazi Germany—but there was also a civil war between Serbs and Croats going on. In other words, there was a recorded history of bloodshed in our country, and it was easy to manipulate it in order to antagonize one another: Serbs became the enemies of Croats, Bosnian Muslims, and Albanians, and the Croats at one point were also at war not only with Serbs but with Muslims as well, while the Macedonians' enemies were Albanians.

Even if it appeared that way to us, the war did not descend upon us overnight. In the late eighties communism collapsed everywhere in Eastern Europe and in what was then still the Soviet Union. Yugoslavia was unprepared for the political changes that followed that collapse. We did not develop any democratic alternatives as Poland and Czechoslovakia had done, and the political vacuum was suddenly filled with nationalist parties. They all had the same program: independence and nation-states of their own.

Simmering nationalism was soon spreading like a fire. The nationalist parties were voted into power in Croatia and Bosnia. In Serbia something strange happened: the Communist Party turned nationalist, led by Slobodan Milošević, who believed this was the way to keep his grip on power. Soon there were referendums all over, and people were voting for their independence from Yugoslavia. Slovenia took the first step, and by June 1991 it was out of the federation. The breakup had begun. The JNA (Yugoslav National Army) tried to stop Slovenia from leaving, but because Slovenia had no minorities to speak of, the army let it go.

At this point, war did not look like a possibility. The names of the few soldiers and policemen killed in that spring of 1991 in Slovenia and Croatia were still noticed: their deaths were still exceptional, and their photos and names were printed on the front pages of newspapers.

But Croatia had a large Serbian minority, thus Slobodan Milošević, as president of Serbia, had the perfect excuse to send his army to "protect" the Serbs there. That meant real war. In the autumn of 1991, the Croatian town of Vukovar was almost erased from the face of the earth, and some ten thousand people lost their lives. In the years that followed, death became an ordinary thing, and nobody bothered anymore to list the victims' names. It was too late for that.

In Bosnia, where Serbs, Croats, and Muslims lived together, the war started in April 1992. Because of the mixed population, it also took on the characteristics of a civil war. The Serbian minority there, "protected" by Milošević, proclaimed the independent state of Republika Srpska. Not being able to prevent either Croatia or Bosnia from leaving Yugoslavia, Milošević—together with Serbs from Republika Srpska— now embarked on a war for a "Great Serbia." The two-year siege of Sarajevo followed, and a couple of years later, the UN-protected Muslim enclave of Srebrenica fell to the army of Republika Srpska. Some seven thousand unarmed Muslim men were executed—the biggest massacre in Europe since 1945.

As these newly created states at war—Bosnia, Croatia, Republika Srpska, Serbia—were led by hard-core nationalist leaders, it was soon clear that they were fighting not only for independence but also for "ethnically cleansed" nation-states. Entire regions in Croatia and Bosnia—and, later on, in Kosovo as well—were ethnically cleansed (a euphemism that in practice often meant genocide) in order to achieve a homogeneous population, not unlike Hitler's Germany of "Ein Reich, ein Volk, ein Führer." Both Serbs and Croats wanted to carve up Bosnia between themselves, leaving only small enclaves to the Muslims.

The war in Bosnia ended with the Dayton Agreement of November 1995, but it was not yet finished in Kosovo, a southern province of Serbia populated mainly by Albanians.

They too wanted independence and began to fight for it. Milošević's retaliation was such that at one point hundreds of thousands of Albanians left their homes in panic in order not to be killed and tried to cross the border into Albania or Macedonia. With at least seven hundred thousand refugees leaving Kosovo, it was a humanitarian disaster. At that point, in the spring of 1999, NATO decided to bomb Milošević into submission.

This was the beginning of the end of Slobodan Milošević. In October 2000 the unimaginable happened: Milošević lost the elections—and his power. He was soon arrested and delivered to the International Criminal Tribunal for the former Yugoslavia (ICTY) in The Hague. This tribunal had been formed in 1993 in the Netherlands, after the international community realized that the new states that had come out of the war were unable or unwilling to prosecute their war criminals themselves. As was stated at the tribunal, all sides committed war crimes, but Serbia committed most of them. Arresting and extraditing war criminals became the biggest political issue in Croatia, Serbia, and Bosnia, where persons now listed in The Hague as war criminals were hailed as national heroes at home.

Today there are some eighty people being prosecuted at the tribunal, from all of the sides in the war. My choice of characters in this book is a personal, not a representative, one. My interest is centered not only on the most important alleged war criminals, like Slobodan Milošević, but also on those whose cases or personalities I found relevant to the purpose of this book, regardless of nationality. That there are no Muslim war criminals described at any length in this book is therefore just a coincidence; it certainly doesn't mean that they did not commit crimes of that type; you can see their names on the ICTY list of wanted men. I also describe two persons who have not been on trial at the tribunal but who are nevertheless important for understanding the issues at hand. One is a witness, Milan Levar; the other is Slobodan Milošević's wife, Mirjana Mira Marković.

My interest in writing this book was a simple one: as it cannot be denied that war crimes were committed, I wanted to find out about the people who committed them. Who were they? Ordinary people like you or me—or monsters?

And to answer the question I originally raised: why didn't we see the war coming? Certainly we could see the writing on the wall. There were many signs of the coming disaster, yet we were not capable of reading them properly until it was too late. But it is easy to be wise in hindsight. Could the war have been prevented? Perhaps. But too few people tried to do so.

CHAPTER I

Why The Hague

FOR SOME time after the war in Croatia was over—although it was still in progress in Bosnia—a young man who was a friend of my daughter stayed in our house in Zagreb. I noticed that he didn't switch off the light in his room at night. When I asked him why, he told me, briefly. He might wake up during the night not knowing where he was. He might have bad dreams—dreams about his friends, soldiers who had disappeared in action in Bosnia and were very probably killed. But he would say no more than this.

Now he has a family and a baby girl, and I am sure he will never tell her about his friends. But if she does grow up hearing his stories about the war in Bosnia, she will be confused. In school she will probably learn that, officially, Croatia was never at war with Bosnia, was never an aggressor. Officially, her father was not fighting against Muslims in Bosnia, and his friends were not killed there either. If the history textbooks of today are any indication, the girl may be taught that the war for the homeland—as it is called—was a defensive war and nothing more. Moreover, *because* it was a defensive war, Croatian soldiers could not have committed war crimes.

At least this has been the official doctrine in Croatia for the past ten years, and it did not change with the death of the first Croatian president, Franjo Tudjman, in 1999.

A girl in Serbia will probably also grow up amid denial about the war. If she should ask her father about the war in Croatia or in Bosnia, he might reply: War? What war? The only wars Serbs recognize are the NATO war against them and their own war against "terrorism" in Kosovo. The wars in Croatia and Bosnia do not count for them.

This is how I imagine my father must have felt after the war in 1945: exactly like my daughter's friend. I don't know if he kept the light in his room on, but my father was twenty-three years old and wanted to forget all the terrible experiences he had had during the five years of war. The bad times were behind him. Soon he met my mother, and they started a family. I was born in 1949. The future looked bright.

My father never spoke about the four years he fought as a Partisan under the command of Josip Broz Tito in World War II. He wanted to forget it, and for a long time I saw this as a sign of sanity and self-preservation. "A human being survives by his ability to forget," Varlam Shalamov writes in *Kolyma Tales*. But I knew that even though he did not speak about it, my father must have remembered the war. It was the single most important period in his life, and he must have been marked by it much more than I have been marked by the recent war in the former Yugoslavia. He fought; I did not. And the more I think about it, the more I am convinced that the combination of his silence and the official version of the historical events of 1939–45 made this latest war possible.

Although my father did not talk about what he saw or experienced, there are three images that I, as a child, used to connect with that war—with his war. The first comes from my grandmother. She also spent the war with the Partisan army, cooking and washing for them, and she often recounted an episode from that time that was fixed in her memory. The Partisans had recaptured a Croatian village that had been held earlier by Serbian Chetniks. The village was empty now, the people had fled. As my grandmother entered a deserted house she planned to stay in overnight, she noticed a strange smell. It was the smell of burned meat. The Chetniks had left in haste, and she was convinced that there was some food burning on the stove. But there was no food there. She opened the oven. Inside it she found a newborn child roasted like a piglet.

When I was small, I used to imagine my grandma entering that house. I could sense that strange smell, even though I had never smelled it. In my mind I could see a black iron stove fed by logs in front of me and her hand opening it. I could imagine her horror, too. With time, her horror became mine.

The second image stuck in my mind is one I saw in a movie entitled *Kozara,* but to me it was real. I was thirteen. I remember well the fear I felt while I watched it, my perspiration, sweaty palms, tears. It was one of those obligatory movies about Tito's Partisan battles with the German army that our history teacher took us to see. There is a scene in which the hero—a Partisan, of course—is hiding in a hole in the ground. German soldiers are looking for him. They are coming closer and closer. He can hear them shouting. In his arms he holds a small child; as the enemy soldiers approach, the child starts crying. The hero closes the baby's mouth with one hand. With the other hand he holds up the make-shift roof of the hole. In the most breathtaking moment of the film, a German soldier stabs at the earth with his bayonet, trying to find the hero's hiding place, and cuts through the palm of the hero's hand.

My third image of the war comes from a book that my father tried to keep away from us children, but I managed to get hold of it anyway. It would have been better if I had not, because I could not ask father about what I saw in it, and it took me a long time to understand what the frightening images in the book were about. I remember the book quite distinctly. It was a slim volume of yellowish paper with a green cloth cover. Inside there were a few black-and-white photos. They were of poor quality, not very clear. But they were clear enough that I could see emaciated people sitting or lying on bunk beds, naked skeletons, and heaps of corpses on the ground. The title of the book was *Jasenovac*. Years later, when I visited the museum of the concentration camp near Jasenovac, I saw the same pictures. I also saw a collection of knives and hammers that the Ustashe, Croatian fascists, used to kill some seventy thousand people. Twenty thousand of them were Jews; the others were Serbs, Gypsies, and Croatian Communists.

We grew up with many such images, gathered from movies, literature, and family stories. On the one hand we had memory, but on the other hand we had our history textbooks, which shaped history to suit the Communist Party ideology. It was not that we were sheltered from the past; on the contrary, we may have had too much of it. But our history books were filled not with facts but with legends: with Tito's army offensives, his great battles, and his even greater victories. Decades later, when I learned about the big massacre that had taken place in the spring of 1945 near Bleiburg in Austria, where tens of thousands of soldiers of the fascist Independent State of Croatia, in retreat and considering surrendering to the Allies, were killed mercilessly by Tito's antifascist army, it was too late to recondition me. I already had a very clear idea that Partisans were antifascist heroes, unlike the Chetniks, Germans, and Ustashe. At that point, no historic facts that I learned about with astonishment later on could erase the pictures embedded in my early childhood memory about who were the good guys and who were the bad ones. It must have been the same for people whose uncle or father was killed there by Partisans. They too grew up with memories of these relatives while knowing that their slaughter was not even mentioned in the history books. My generation grew up never learning history—history as we knew it was a lie, a deceit.

Only now can I understand how easy it is to start a war in the absence of facts. War does not come from nowhere; I saw in Yugoslavia that it must be prepared. It is easy for political leaders to use images like the ones that I remember, to use people's emotional memory and build hatred upon it. Because in totalitarian societies, where there is no true history, each person has in his own memory a collection of such images, and it becomes dangerous if he has nothing more than that. Political leaders can appeal to these images, mix them with popular mythology, and stir emotions by repeating propaganda endlessly on television. One can hardly defend oneself against such propaganda if there is no common history that everybody can believe in. Under the pressure of emotions, a thin layer of rationality easily falls away. The history that we learned—which was not in fact history— made it easier for us to abandon reason in favor of pure emotions.

So when I experienced the same silence, the same absence of a desire for truth, and the same kind of manipulation of facts after the end of the war in 1995, I became afraid. This was the third time I was confronted with the "ground zero" of history. First it happened with my father's generation after World War II, that is, after the Communist revolution. All the history that went before was rewritten. The second time it happened was after the collapse of communism, when we had to forget about communism and start counting time (and writing history) from the year 1990. And the third time is now, after the end of the last war. In Croatia it is easy to perceive the general unwillingness to talk about the war at all, almost as if it had never happened. It is even easier to conclude that people are tired of it and want to leave the past behind and think of the future. After all, thinking of the past got them into the war in the first place. Politicians are all too happy to join the majority of the people and preach the message of "turning a new page of history"—blank, if possible—

because many of them are still in power and don't want to accept the responsibility for a past war.

Yet if the truth is not established about the war for the homeland, the next generation will one day find itself in exactly the same situation as my post–Second World War generation. All they will have to rely upon will be dusty images and bloody stories. These will vary, depending on which side their parents were on, but they will be left with only memory, not history.

And the war is still with us. One need only mention The Hague to see that. I guess that every Dutchman would be astonished by the strong emotions provoked in Croatia, Serbia, and even Bosnia (because Bosnia is more cooperative with the tribunal) by the mention of this pretty Dutch city. Ever since 1993, when the International Criminal Tribunal for the former Yugoslavia was established there, The Hague has been a source of controversy in the Balkans. The ICTY was established because the former Yugoslav states were either unable or unwilling to prosecute their own war criminals. Far from being independent, their judicial systems were deeply corrupt, and there would have been enormous political pressure if alleged war criminals were tried in local courts. Back home in Croatia, this argument immediately became fiercely disputed. Opponents of the International Tribunal on the right argued that the ICTY court was a political instrument established to punish and humiliate their country. The more sophisticated critics argued that it would be better to hold the trials for war criminals at home, because it would give the nation a way to face the truth about the war and experience a catharsis.

I was naïve enough to believe that one of the priorities of the new post-Tudjman government would be to try to face the truth about the war: why did it happen? What was it about? Did the Croatian army commit war crimes or not? It is, of course, a hard truth: the war was about forming a nation-state with ethnic cleansing; 200,000 Serbs were forced to leave Krajina; their homes were burned and plundered; some 400 civilians were killed; Serb civilians in Gospić, Pakrac, and Sisak were executed en masse; 24,000 Muslims were detained by Bosnian Croatian soldiers in forty-four concentration camps in Herzegovina; Croats killed 116 civilians in the village of Ahmici and blew up the old bridge in Mostar; in 1991, in Zagreb, a twelve-year-old girl named Aleksandra Zec was killed, along with her Serbian parents. Her murderer, who confessed, is nevertheless still at large.

However, nobody wants to say this truth out loud. Nor, for that matter, does anybody want to hear it. This is because the truth in Croatia is dangerous. For ten years Tudjman's propaganda convinced Croats that people on the tribunal's list of war criminals—like Mladen Naletilić Tuta, Tihomir Blaškić, Dario Kordić, Mirko Norac, and Ante Gotovina—should be seen as heroes. If Tudjman's government extradited them, it was only because of serious international pressure, not because Croats believed they should be tried. But how is it possible for the views from the inside and those from the outside to be so conflicting? It is possible because

Croats were never told that these men were "willing executioners," even if they were war heroes. So when these men
are suspected by The Hague of either killing or ordering the
killing of civilians, Croats are offended. Their heroes are war
criminals? Never! To stand up against the tribunal became a
sign of patriotism. The opponents of the tribunal claim that
it is trying not individuals but the whole of Croatia for war
crimes. When in the spring of 2001 Mirko Norac was ordered
to appear in a local court in Rijeka on suspicion of committing war crimes in Gospić, where more than one hundred
Serbs disappeared in the autumn of 1991, war veterans organized a protest meeting in Split. Some seventy-five thousand
people attended that meeting. The government was in crisis
and the country paralyzed for at least a week.

Establishing the truth about the war is at the heart of the
controversies surrounding The Hague tribunal. Until the
truth about the war is established, trials of the war criminals,
whether in the International Tribunal or in the local courts,
will be experienced as an injustice to the "war heroes." There
is no justice without truth, and Croatia is still far from such
truth. Recently there were two trials of war criminals: one of
the "Gospić group" in Rijeka and the other of a group of
prison guards in Split. The trial in Split in particular has de-
generated into a shameful performance, with the public ap-
plauding their "heroes" and threatening the witnesses. The
judge let the defendants out of prison, but a superior court
reversed the decision, only to realize that two defendants
had escaped in the meantime. Witnesses in both trials are

prone to sudden losses of memory. Or, in the case of Sisak, a small town near Zagreb from which a large number of Serbian civilians disappeared in 1991 and 1992, a local judge did not order an investigation until ten years later and then only under pressure from the media, especially the magazine *Hrvatska ljevica*, which published a list of some hundred killed and "disappeared" persons.

In this Croatia is not alone. Serbs also have problems with the truth. In their eyes, they, the Serbs, are the biggest victims of both Milošević and NATO. Indeed, the Serbian society has suffered severe consequences—from embargoes to NATO bombing—as a result of the wars it waged against its neighbors, but the whole truth about what happened has not yet surfaced or become part of the public debate. Serbia and Croatia in this respect share a consensus on lies of the past ten years. The reason is a simple one, one that goes beyond the Tudjman-Milošević ideology. Too many people were in some way involved in the war, and too many profited from it. It is easier, and much more comfortable, to live with lies than to confront the truth and with that truth the possibility of individual guilt—and collective responsibility.

However, the conflict between truth and justice has serious political consequences: the governments in both Serbia and Croatia have problems with the truth and justifying to their citizens the extradition of those indicted for war crimes to the tribunal in The Hague. Because people find it easier to live with lies than with the truth, attempts to administer justice through the tribunal or even through the local courts are experienced as an injustice. And as long as there is so little desire in these societies to uncover the truth, justice for war criminals will continue to be perceived as a threat to the entire community. Justice simply has to come from The Hague or it will not come at all—and all because we ourselves are not capable of washing our own dirty, bloody laundry. We do not even realize yet the need to do it.

CHAPTER 2

Justice Is Boring

Inside the tribunal building in Churchill Square in The Hague, it smells of fresh paint. A young man dressed in white overalls is slowly painting the entrance hall, which is otherwise empty and has big glass walls on either side. On the left is the entrance door to the offices of the court, with a metal detector and a policeman, of course. I want to go to courtroom number three, where the trials of Miroslav Kvočka, Dragoljub Prćac, Milojica Kos, Mladjo Radić, and Zoran Žigić are taking place; all of them are accused of murder and torture in the Omarska and Keraterm camps in Bosnia. A second metal detector is at the top of the marble staircase. Once I pass it (no tape recorders or cameras allowed in the courtroom), I climb up a narrow metal staircase to the courtroom, where yet another policeman stands at the door. Courtroom number three is rather small and is divided in half by a bulletproof glass wall. In the space for the public, about a hundred persons can be seated in uncomfortable blue plastic chairs. There are two TV screens in each corner. It doesn't look like the courtrooms in the movies and TV shows like *L.A. Law,* with their dark wood paneling.

This courtroom looks more like a waiting room in a hospital: aseptic, with simple, functional furniture and gray wall-to-wall carpeting and lit with strong neon lights that make people look pale and sickly.

I sit in the first row because I want a clear view. But I can sit anywhere I please, because I am the entire public today. I am a bit surprised—admission is free—but it seems that there is not much interest in the daily proceedings of the trials. I have been told that law students and relatives of the defendants come here from time to time but journalists come only at the opening of a trial and when a sentence is to be delivered. Then it is hardly possible to squeeze yourself in. Now I am facing the three judges sitting on a kind of platform; the defendants and their lawyers are to my left and the prosecution lawyers to my right. The defendants can see the public through the glass; only a few meters separate us. The glass wall was probably put there to protect them from a possible assault. But it feels to me as though *I* am the one being protected from the dangerous men behind it.

So I sit and watch them, the five defendants. They look so common. But what did I expect to see? Horns? Pointed ears? After all, they were just ordinary policemen, except for Žigić, who was a taxi driver. Interestingly enough, he is the only one who looks threatening, maybe because he has a stronger build than the other four. Žigić is a dark man in his forties with a broad neck, dressed in a brown suit and yellow shirt. Today his defense witness is being examined. Next to him is Prćac, an elderly man, gray haired and thin. In his gray suit and with his small grayish moustache, he looks like a mouse.

The two of them sit between two UN policemen, who look as if they are thinking of last Sunday's picnic. Seated behind them, also flanked by two UN policemen, is the rest of the group: Kos and Kvočka give the impression of village troublemakers, while stocky Radić looks as if he could be a factory director in a too small town.

Žigić is nervously shifting back and forth in his chair, as though he wants to smoke a cigarette. Surely he smokes; most Bosnian men do. He probably wants a cup of coffee, too: in Bosnia they drink a strong coffee that used to be called Turkish coffee. I wonder what the politically correct term is now: Serbian coffee? The five men sit there, day after day, for hours without either cigarettes or coffee, listening to the translation of what the lawyers and judges are saying. Sometimes they must feel as if they are in a movie. Probably they never expected to end up in a court abroad. And what is now happening to them is so unreal that they expect the scene to fade out at any moment.

One of the judges is now examining a protected witness for the defense. A protected witness cannot be seen by the public; he sits behind plastic blinds, and his face is shown, distorted, on a TV screen. This trial has been going on for almost a year now, and if you are in the courtroom for the first time, as I am, it is not easy to follow what is happening. Not because of the topic at hand but because of the procedure. A witness may be examined in minute detail, and it is easy to become lost if you don't keep in mind what it is all about. Often there are procedural questions that have to be clarified, which makes it even more difficult for an observer. This witness had been a guard in the Keraterm camp, and he was there on the night of July 24, 1992, when a massacre in one of the barracks took place in which more than one hundred prisoners were killed. This is how the cross-examination goes:

> *Judge:* Did you ever enter the room with prisoners?
> *Witness:* No.
> *Judge:* Were you near the entrance to that room? How can you tell the diameter of this barrel in front of room number one?
> *Witness:* The doors were open, you could see inside.
> *Judge:* The barrel was inside or outside?
> *Witness:* It was outside.
> *Judge:* How do you know that the diameter was thirty centimeters?
> *Witness:* I estimated it.

I try to follow this for some time, not sure why it is so important to establish where the barrel was but trusting the judge that it is important. However, I catch myself growing bored. I look at the accused. Žigić is trying hard to concentrate; after all, this is a witness for his defense. But one can tell by the expression on his face that he is not listening carefully. His eyes are wandering around the courtroom as mine are. Kos is looking at the ceiling. Prćac seems to be devoting his attention to the woman whose job it is to write down every word, maybe because of the lively flower pattern of her dress. One of the defense lawyers is discreetly yawning.

The cross-examination is long, careful, and exhausting. I

admire the evident concentration of the judges, since I myself feel that I may fall asleep at any moment. Now, after spending some time in this courtroom, I understand why it is empty. A trial—every trial, not only this one—is painstakingly slow and boring. But this is exactly as it should be. A trial is not a show for the audience. It does not need to be interesting or entertaining. It is a serious thing: justice is in question, human lives are at stake, and there is nothing spectacular in proving someone's guilt or innocence.

I look at my watch. Only an hour has passed, but it feels like an eternity to me, as if time has a different quality in this courtroom, as if it is passing more slowly in here than outside in the streets of The Hague. Perhaps it is. I try to focus again. The guard is attempting to defend Žigić, who took part in the massacre. The killing, he says, happened because prisoners tried to escape and were shot while running away. But why the blood in the room? asks the judge. Why the blood on the walls?

Blood on the walls?

Suddenly I see that picture in front of my eyes, and I realize what the judge is talking about. The death of 120 prisoners is no longer an abstraction, no longer mere words. Now the tedious, precise interrogation takes on a new meaning. Now I realize how much we are all poisoned by the trials depicted in television shows and Hollywood movies, with their rapid exchanges of arguments between good-looking lawyers in expensive suits. In The Hague there is no such drama. The drama here is that everything really happened: there were real deaths, real victims, and real murderers. Real blood. The drama is that there can be no escape from that reality. When at the end of that day in the court I take a long look at the defendants, they suddenly seem different to me. I see what I did not see before, not their dull faces but a room with walls splashed with blood.

CHAPTER 3

A Suicide Scenario

Milan Levar, a Croatian war veteran from Gospić and a witness to war crimes, was murdered on August 28, 2000. After the trial of the Gospić group a decade later, his suspected murderer, Ivica Rožić, was released because there was not enough material evidence against him.

IN GOSPIĆ, a decade after the end of the war in Croatia, the war is not over, at least not for Vesna and Leon Levar. If they leave their house, they have to report to the police where they are going. A police patrol will accompany them on their outing. Before they are allowed to visit the grave of their husband and father, Milan Levar, the police thoroughly check the graveyard. The people from Gospić do not talk to Vesna, and boys do not play football with the eleven-year-old Leon. Vesna and Leon belong to the "enemy" camp. This is very unusual in a small town of only six thousand inhabitants, especially because neither Vesna nor Leon has committed a crime. They do not even have the "wrong" (Serbian) blood in their veins; there are very few Serbs living in Gospić nowadays. They are prisoners of war of a very special kind.

"At the mass, a year after my husband's death, we were the only ones in church. And at the grave; not a single representative of the government was there," Vesna has said. But someone visited Milan Levar's grave before her, before the funeral; she found a flower there. A single plastic flower but nevertheless a flower, a sign that someone cared about him. Only that person did not have the courage to be seen at his grave. That person was afraid because the case has not been solved yet, and the murderer is still at large. Newspapers say that the police know who the murderer is, but they do not have enough evidence to arrest him.

Milan Levar was the first witness for the tribunal to be killed in revenge. A single walk along the streets of Gospić and one begins to understand how much the spirit of the province contributed to the murder of Levar. It takes only about half an hour to see the entire town. Like the people, all the buildings that are left standing bear the deep scars of war: dilapidated houses with facades peeling off like burned skin and shattered windows, empty ruins, and pockmarked streets. One cannot escape the sight of gaping walls exposing the ravaged insides of what were once cozy, welcoming, solid brick homes. Their walls are blackened by fire now, fires that were ignited not only by the enemy's shells but also by the neighbors. There are ruins everywhere, monuments to the two months in the autumn of 1991 when thousands of shells fell on the town from the Serbian side. To wake up every day to see those ruins and remember the houses as they were before; this alone must be enough to drive the people of Gospić to madness.

In the main street, men walk unshaved and dressed in fatigues as if the war is still going on for them, as indeed it is for the Levar family. There is not much to do for them in this half-dead place nowadays, so they drink coffee and *rakija*, talk local politics, and wait for something to happen. Everyone who was able left a long time ago, before the war started. People do not come back; there is nothing to come back to. Ten years ago Gospić was a pleasant if sleepy place, where people lived quiet, comfortable lives and children could play safely in the streets. If you so much as sneezed, your neighbor would be there ready to help you. Until that same neighbor came to arrest you.

Now, as you enter the town, you instantly feel what it is that dominates life here: fear. There are few people and they know everything about each other. They know what their neighbors are cooking for lunch, from which deserted or ruined house their carpet, refrigerator, or television comes, and what each of them did during the war. They have good reason to be afraid of each other. It has to do with the TV set syndrome. If you mention this, people will know exactly what you mean. It means that a majority of them used the war to help themselves to TV sets and similar goods from deserted houses. There are others who did far worse things, of course, but if one dares to challenge them and demand justice, they will say: "You shut up, you stole a TV set." As if killing a man can ever be equated with stealing a TV. Of course it cannot, but the comparison is enough to keep mouths shut.

Which brings us to the next thing you notice in Gospić:

silence. Indeed, there is a conspiracy of silence, something like the Italian *omertà,* the law of silence of the Sicilian Mafia. Such a dangerous, threatening silence is obvious in a place that is small enough. Of course it is not really silent; cars drive past, babies cry, people talk, and loud music fills the cafés. The suffocating silence falls only when you attempt to talk about certain subjects. For example, nobody wants to talk about what happened to Serbian civilians in October 1991 or about why Milan Levar was killed. If somebody does comment on his death, it is most likely a curse. "He should have been killed sooner. He is a traitor, and thank God somebody liquidated him," said a neighbor in a matter-of-fact way only a few hours after his funeral.

You really must be exceptionally hated to evoke such cruel, cynical words even after your death. Levar was such a person. In a provincial town where differences are abhorred, he dared to be different. He believed that justice could be done and that it was worth fighting for. Moreover, Levar believed that he could testify in court about the atrocities committed against Serbian civilians in Gospić during the war and still live a normal life among some of the very people who got their hands dirty, whether they did so by arresting Serbs, digging their graves, stealing furniture, or just closing their eyes and refusing to see what was happening. But Levar was not allowed to do this. He knew their secrets, so he became a threat to them all, a critic of their way of life and their cowardly behavior.

He should have known better. Their hatred was palpable. He must have felt it every time he walked out of his home.

He must have seen it on the faces of people who passed him every day. For his family, going shopping must have been like going on an expedition through hostile territory. If anyone offered sympathy, it was secretly, under the cover of night. How would they ever survive besieged by curses and threats? His wife, Vesna, endured offensive remarks every day when she was at work earning their main, albeit meager, income. And their little boy, Leon—how many times was he called a "Chetnik's bastard" by his schoolmates? This hatred must have worn them out sometimes. They were not made of steel. It must have been even more painful for Levar because he had been born in Gospić; it was his hometown. And yet he was convinced that he could be strong enough to fight the provincial lethargy and fear.

His biggest mistake was not his decision to tell the truth and become a witness; it was his belief that he could go on living in Gospić after that. It was a suicide scenario. It was not possible to live among the very people he wanted to put behind bars, especially since some of those people were still in power. Instead of investigating war crimes, they covered them up. They had their own reasons to do so, and Levar knew it.

But what happened in Gospić that winter? What was it that Milan Levar witnessed? What was it that he ultimately paid for so dearly?

In the autumn of 1991 two men from Zagreb were put in charge of the defense of Gospić, although it is not clear by whom; such were the times. Perhaps they took charge of the defense themselves. They were Tihomir Orešković, who became the head of the provisional civil government, and Mirko Norac, who became the head of military defense. Their names are worth remembering. They defended the town successfully against the Serbian attack (though some people say that they only arrived after the battle for Gospić was over). They also understood that the aim of the war was to clean the town of the unwanted Serbs. This was a good opportunity. In the heated atmosphere of war it was enough to proclaim a person as suspected of collaborating with the enemy. No proof was necessary. They composed a list of Serbian civilians still living in the town. In three days, from the sixteenth to the eighteenth of October, more than one hundred Serbs and some forty Croats disappeared. According to several eyewitness accounts that surfaced later—not just that of Levar—the Serbian civilians were taken by truck to locations outside Gospić, where they were executed by the military police squad under the command of Norac and buried in hidden mass graves.

For what followed there is no other word but plundering. The deserted houses, not only of the murdered Serbs but also of those who had fled the town earlier, were ransacked and burned. There were very few people who did not take part in this. It was the beginning of a reign of terror led by a small group of followers of Orešković and Norac. They did exactly as they pleased, deciding who should live and who should die while accumulating wealth in dubious ways. Because almost no one in Gospić was innocent of the events in October 1991, everybody kept silent. And even if there were innocent people among them, they most certainly didn't dare to speak. It was easy to rule in a place where everyone had to conform if he wanted to stay alive.

In this deserted town on the front line, Orešković and Norac usurped all the power, and there was nobody to challenge them. "In those times and in the atmosphere of the war euphoria, it was easy to rule desperate people. You had so many empty houses, and you could appropriate anything you wanted from them. You could do whatever you wanted with the few remaining people because both Croats and Serbs ran away, at least those who could," Levar said later.

Milan Levar was disgusted that neither the army nor the police nor anyone from the government tried to stop Orešković and Norac's reign of terror. Together with two of his colleagues from the militia, Zdenko Ropac and Zdenko Banda (who later went into hiding in Germany), he contacted some important people in the Croatian government and informed them of the situation in Gospić. Levar knew what he was talking about: he himself had been forced by Orešković at gunpoint to watch while a Serb civilian was strangled with a telephone cord.

The authorities in Zagreb knew what was going on almost immediately because the relatives of those who had disappeared had also contacted various people in the government. The government was forced to start an investigation. Ante Karić, the president of the Crisis Council in Zagreb, was sent to Gospić at the beginning of November 1991. He returned with a detailed report of the usurpation of power by the military police. People had disappeared overnight, the black market flourished, the deserted houses of both Croats and Serbs were in ruins. This report was sent to both President Franjo Tudjman and the chief of the secret police, Josip Manolić. Again someone was dispatched to Gospić by the Office for Defense of Constitutional Order. In a report dated December 20, 1991, Rikard Pavelić described the atmosphere of terror, the mysterious disappearances of people, the discovery of new corpses every day, the plundering and looting—all connected to the military police. "For the majority of liquidated people there are witnesses that the military police took them away to Perušić and other places, where all traces of them are lost," wrote Pavelić. "People are taken away daily and new corpses are found." The chief of police in Gospić, Ivan Dasović, was there when a large group of Serbian civilians were liquidated. Not only did he list the people who took part in the decision making, but he himself, as he later confessed, was at the execution site, shooting, while the commanding officer, Norac, was shouting, "Shoot, shoot, what are you waiting for?"

The Croatian government and the president were informed of what was happening in Gospić, and there was enough proof of war crimes. Something needed to be done, so Orešković was arrested. He and several other people from Gospić were brought to Zagreb and investigated. But after the intervention of the minister of defense, Gojko Šušak, the investigation was suspended and Orešković was released. Šušak had enormous influence on Tudjman, and, though aware of their crimes, Tudjman agreed that it was better not to take action against Orešković and Norac.

When Levar and his companions realized that their reports to the authorities had achieved nothing but danger for themselves, they left the militia. One can only try to imagine Levar's despair. But why did he not leave Gospić? Was it his stubborn nature that kept him there? Did he have some hidden motives? Those who knew him say that Milan Levar was an honest man, a man of principle; he did not want the new state of Croatia to be built on war crimes. But others claim that he was deranged by the war. In an interview with the independent weekly of Split, the *Feral Tribune,* in 1996, Levar said: "Lika [the region of Gospić] today is ruled by fear. In order for this fear to disappear, people have to, finally, account for their deeds. It has to be established who killed and who stole, and everyone has to bear the consequences. Because in this way those who committed crimes, by keeping all power in their hands, turned us into prisoners and are treating us as slaves."

The problem was that the government itself was part of the conspiracy. Nobody wanted to investigate the case; it would not look good for it to become known that not just Serbs but Croats as well had committed war crimes. There was political reasoning behind hiding the truth about Gospić. This was a time when Croatia was fighting for international recognition as an independent state. The truth about the murder of the Serbian civilians in Gospić might impede that recognition. It was better to cover up the whole unpleasant affair. So, the truth was buried in the name of "higher" (political) interests. Those in power in Gospić were entrusted with keeping its secrets.

Levar came to realize that only public opinion could reverse the situation. If he could manage to muster enough popular support, the government would have to investigate Orešković and Norac again. However, when Levar told *Globus* magazine what he had witnessed, the only result was threats.

Silence shrouded the whole Gospić case until 1996, when Tihomir Orešković finally tried to establish power in the Lika region by putting himself forward as a candidate for mayor of the town of Perušić. Once more Levar went to the newspapers, to the *Feral Tribune*. He got more publicity this time; even foreign newspapers picked up on the Gospić case. But again the outcome was not what Levar had hoped for: the investigation was not reopened, although Orešković did withdraw his candidacy.

The public pressure Levar hoped to create did not manifest itself. Indeed, the general public seemed to be indifferent to his story. It was as if everybody, not just in Gospić but in the whole of Croatia, were deaf and blind. Perhaps people were blinded by the "national interest," but it is as likely that there were other, more personal, interests at stake. This time both Levar and Zdenko Banda were explicitly threatened. Explosives were found in Levar's mother's house and in Banda's summer home in Karlobag. The message was loud and clear: stop talking or else.

Bitter and disappointed, Levar was left with little choice but to turn to the ICTY in The Hague. He had tried everything else, from offering his statement to the Croatian governmental institutions to attempting to bring the whole affair out into the open through the newspapers, to no avail. He gave his sworn testimony to the tribunal in 1997 and

1998. He believed that his statement in The Hague would finally force the Croatian government to begin a real investigation of the Gospić case.

People working at the tribunal knew very well what Levar's testimony meant and how dangerous it was. They also knew that there would no longer be a life for Levar in Gospić after he had been proclaimed a traitor. So they offered to make him a protected witness, to move him and his family abroad and give them new identities. But Levar turned down the offer, believing that going public would give him enough protection. He thought that if he stayed, his presence would motivate other people to be witnesses as well. He could not let them down by leaving Croatia. But he was naïve, as if he had forgotten that he was dealing with murderers. He also had too much confidence in the Croatian legal system. Two other witnesses, his former colleagues Zdenko Banda and Zdenko Ropac, did not think twice; they left for Germany.

The tribunal still wanted to help Levar so it demanded protection for him from the Croatian government. But was this demand passed on to the local police in Gospić? Even if it had been, would the Gospić police have protected a man who was willing to give evidence about crimes committed by the military police in collaboration with the civilian police forces? Not much had changed after the war; the same people were still there. For them, Levar was a man who knew too much and talked too much. He had been warned several times and surely had gotten the message. Now he was in a serious dilemma—but it did not stop him talking.

The elections and the change of government in January 2000 must have brought him new hope, but that hope did not last long. Months passed, but there still was no investigation into the Gospić case or any other war crimes cases for that matter. Levar must have been terribly disappointed and thought about leaving Croatia. "Lately, Milan changed his mind and wanted to leave Croatia," Vesna recalled, crying. "I will never forgive myself for being against that."

Seven months later, on the afternoon of August 28, 2000, Milan Levar was killed by a bomb. It happened in his mother's yard. The bomb was hidden in the spare tire of his car. His son, Leon, was there. He tried to help his father, wanted to turn him onto his back, but it was too late. "He called me on the mobile telephone but could not say anything. He was just screaming," said his mother. Nobody in Gospić was surprised that Levar was killed. The town was too small for someone labeled a traitor to survive. There was no place there to hide. Being a witness in Gospić, living among six thousand people, was far riskier than being a witness in Zagreb, a city with a million inhabitants.

It was silence that slowly killed Milan Levar over the years, not just a bomb. The silence of neighbors, of friends, of the province, of public opinion, as well as the cover-up of the government in Zagreb. This should have changed when Levar made all those crimes public. What he hoped for was that once the war crimes became public knowledge, there would be no way back to feigned ignorance and indifference.

But what do you do if you reveal a crime and nothing happens? No reaction. No pressure. Just a blanket of silence, even more suffocating than what you felt at the time the events in Gospić took place. Levar had not expected this. He did not understand the apathy of the people in Croatia, that they simply did not want to hear him and purposely ignored facts even when they were laid out before them. He had miscalculated, and he must have asked himself why. The answer is the same as for what happened in the town of Gospić. Too many people profited from ethnic cleansing in many different, sometimes only small, ways. Moreover, even those who did not profit did not protest either. There were some people who supported Levar and were willing to listen to the truth, but they were too few to make a difference.

To stir up public opinion was his last option. Because this attempt failed so miserably, Levar is dead today. Public opinion is not an abstract concept. It is about us, what we the citizens of Croatia stand for. The failure of public opinion is therefore our failure. We did not react; we have nobody but ourselves to blame. Our personal paranoia, petty theft, and sealed lips all contributed to the bomb that killed Levar.

Not many people came to his funeral. Instead of turning into a mass demonstration in support of the principles he died for, the funeral was just another episode in a long line of betrayals. Some people were afraid to show up; most just did not care. There were no representatives from the military, no politicians, no religious dignitaries, no human rights groups, and no one from the media. Their absence was more significant than their presence would have been.

After Milan Levar was murdered, things became clear.

The police now had no choice but to start an investigation, not only into Levar's murder but into the Gospić case as well.

Ten years after the war crimes were committed, the fear of the surfacing truth is still great. The Croatian state is still indecisive, the international community is indifferent, and public opinion remains silent.

CHAPTER 4

A Quiet Night in October

The trial of the Gospić group was a landmark one for the Croatian legal system. This is because the five men (Tihomir Orešković, Mirko Norac, Stjepan Grandić, Ivica Rožić, and Milan Čanić) were tried for killing Serbs in Gospić in the winter of 1991, not at the ICTY but in the local court in Rijeka. Their trial lasted from June 2001 to March 2003, some 150 witnesses testified, and three of the accused were found guilty of killing fifty people. The other two were acquitted for lack of evidence.

I T WAS already late at night when a military truck stopped on the outskirts of Gospić, near a village called Pazarište. A military policeman lifted the tarp in the back, and some twelve people stepped down onto the damp earth. As they came out of the truck, they saw the silhouettes of armed men waiting for them. They could hear the sound of the truck departing, of car doors opening and closing, of muffled voices and the clanking of arms—and then, for a minute or two, awkward silence. Somebody nervously tried to light a cigarette but gave up, swearing.

Suddenly, a woman's scream pierced the darkness. It was

a high-pitched, short scream followed by a shot and a man's voice: "Shoot, shoot, what are you waiting for?" Then the small group of armed shadows started shooting. Everyone was shooting: soldiers with machine guns, civilians with pistols. It would be dangerous not to, because someone was going from man to man checking if they had fired their weapons. After a few minutes all the people from the back of the truck were dead. Armed men jumped into their cars and left hurriedly. The bodies were never found.

This happened on October 16, 1991, and it was preceded by a meeting in Gospić at the crisis headquarters, organized by Tihomir Orešković, the head of the civilian government, and the one who, according to witnesses, was checking the arms after the shooting. The voice in the dark issuing the command to shoot belonged to Mirko Norac, the military commander of Gospić. Both were put in jail in Rijeka together with four other men from the Gospić group. They were indicted for ordering executions and executing Serbian civilians. The events of the night of October 16 were only the beginning. For the next few years the life of a Serb in Gospić or of a Croat who disagreed with the policy of the local bosses, Orešković and Norac, was worth less than that of a stray dog. A report by a police investigator a year later stated that more than one hundred people disappeared into the mass graves near Gospić in a single night in October.

It is hard to imagine Mirko Norac shouting the order for execution. He does not look like a soldier, much less like a tough war commander. Not even a general's uniform can make him look manly and capable of such a job. A plump, plain young man with a shy smile and a double chin, he looks more soft than dangerous. People who know him say that his most important characteristic is loyalty, and this could be the reason he rose so quickly in the hierarchy of the Croatian army, eventually becoming a general.

Norac actually looks like what he really is, a waiter. It is much easier to imagine him in a café in Sinj, serving coffee and beer to the locals and chatting with them about the scores of Sunday's soccer game. Not that Norac spent much time working as a waiter; he was not at all eager to work—as long as his father sent enough money home from Germany, where he worked on construction sites. Norac was not wild about school either. He barely finished the two years at the school that qualified him as a waiter and later took several courses in a military school. He was considered neither particularly bright nor particularly diligent. In his small village of Otok, near Sinj, it was common for people to become priests or nuns; Otok is famous for having provided 35 men to the priesthood and 170 women who took vows as nuns. Norac's uncle and a nephew are priests, and he himself was a ministrant in the church. There is no mystery here. The people of Otok are no more Catholic than others in Croatia, but in this part of Croatia there is extreme poverty, and men have very few options. One is to become a priest, the other a soldier or a policeman.

Norac might have become a priest, but he became a soldier instead. Providence helped him in this. At twenty-three, jobless and not knowing what to do with himself, in August

1991 he joined the first group of volunteer soldiers and ended up in a special unit near Zagreb.

That autumn, he and three of his friends went to Gospić with the intention of organizing the defense of the town against the Serbian attack. It is not clear whether they were posted there by the-then minister of defense, Gojko Šušak, or if they ended up in Gospić through their own initiative and connections. Information about this is contradictory. It was a chaotic period, and every new trial at the tribunal proves the existence of parallel commands, the official one (the government) and the unofficial one (the HDZ, or Croatian Democratic Union, the party's line of command). While the official history says that Norac organized the defense under his own command and that the Croatian army stabilized the front line, there are witnesses who say that Norac appeared in Gospić to take over power after the town had already been defended by its citizens.

Before the war, Gospić, a town of some six thousand inhabitants, had a mixed population. About 30 percent were Serbs, but most of them left Gospić at the beginning of the war. The task of Norac and Tihomir Orešković, who came with Norac from Zagreb, was not only to defend the town. It was also to ethnically cleanse Gospić; that is, to completely get rid of the Serbs. Was it an order from the very top, by Gojko Šušak or even by the president, Franjo Tudjman? Perhaps there was no need to give such an order at all. Tudjman's political messages were clear enough, and both Norac and Orešković understood that defense was one thing, while the long-term goal of the war in Croatia was quite another. Besides, they were both members of a small radical right-wing emigrant party, the Croatian Statehood Party (HDP).

After Gospić, Norac took part in the Medak pocket action in 1993 and in the Storm action in 1995 in Krajina against the Serbian rebel army. He became the commander of the Knin Corps and the youngest general in the Croatian army. Then the war ended. He continued to live peacefully in Zagreb, enjoying the privileges attached to his high rank and his status as war veteran and hero. He had a nice apartment, a good car, and plenty of money. A waiter from Otok could not have hoped for more.

The years passed until one day, in August 2000, a bomb exploded in a yard in Gospić. That bomb killed Milan Levar, a man who had claimed that the executions in Gospić were not incidental but part of the ethnic cleansing campaign, the actual war strategy of Tudjman's government.

Less than a month afterward, the arrest of five suspects was ordered, and the investigation began in the court in Rijeka. Tihomir Orešković was among those arrested.

But something unexpected happened. The beginning of the investigation of war crimes in Rijeka brought with it a series of protests. The government was aware that public opinion was against extraditing war criminals to the tribunal in The Hague; now it even began to turn against a trial in Croatia itself.

Protests were staged by the organizations of war veterans. Former soldiers perceived both extradition to The Hague and the arrest of the Gospić group as a great injustice. After being treated with respect for defending Croatia against the

Serbian aggressors, they were suddenly under suspicion of committing war crimes. Nobody had told them that what they did—killing Serbian civilians, for example—was wrong. On the contrary, these same men had been awarded decorations, apartments, pensions, and other privileges.

Ten years later the political line in Zagreb changed; what was earlier implicitly approved now had to be investigated. Some war veterans feared that such investigations might implicate them as well. The government was well aware that in many cases war heroes were indeed war criminals, but how to persuade people of this when they had been led to believe that such accusations were unjust and impossible?

The veterans were very loud; they protested against accusing war heroes of committing war crimes. They called this a "shameful criminalization of the war for the homeland." They also suggested that the government should hold a referendum on the question of extradition. Moreover, they openly called for the overthrow of the socialist-dominated coalition government. The leaders of street demonstrations claimed that judging a war hero is humiliating and that trying one puts the whole idea of the war on trial along with the entire Croatian nation. They called this a betrayal of national interests and demanded amnesty for all suspected war criminals.

After the war, the veterans' organizations had grown into a very powerful political instrument controlled by the right-wing Tudjman's HDZ party. Just how powerful an instrument became clear only when they organized demonstrations in Split on March 11, 2001. On that day tens of thousands of people attended a rally in support of former General Mirko

Norac. Some days before this meeting, an order to arrest Norac had been issued. He was supposed to join Tihomir Orešković in a prison in Rijeka. Instead of surrendering to the police, Norac went into hiding.

But why was there such an uproar about Norac? Why are people in Croatia so upset about trials of the war veterans at home—and even more upset about the tribunal in The Hague? Why do Croatians find it so difficult to put on trial or deliver to the tribunal suspected war criminals? Until 2002 Croatia had not extradited any Croats from Croatia proper; Dario Kordić, Tihomir Blaškić, the brothers Kupreškić, Mladen Naletilic Tuta, and Vinko Martinović are all Croats from Bosnia. If they later acquired Croatian citizenship, as they may have done, they fall into a different category. Tudjman delivered these men to the tribunal in The Hague without much resistance from the veterans.

The new post-Tudjman government is no more eager to investigate war crimes than its predecessor, nor is it any more enthusiastic about extraditing Croatian war criminals to the tribunal in The Hague. For a decade Croatian citizens were exposed to Franjo Tudjman's propaganda machine, which claimed that Croatian soldiers defending their country could not be committing war crimes. This was the official doctrine, and everyone accepted it. If there was any investigation at all, the defendants were quickly released because there was not enough evidence against them or because mistakes were made in the course of the investigation (as with the murder of the Serbian Zec family with the twelve-year-old daughter). The new government handed over Rahim

Ademi, a Croatian citizen of Albanian nationality, and there was no reaction from the veterans. But when later on, The Hague asked that another Croatian, also former General Ante Gotovina, be extradited to the tribunal, veterans staged protests. Gotovina went into hiding and has not yet been found. After years of Tudjman's propaganda, it is still difficult and dangerous to admit the truth: that indeed Croatian soldiers could and did commit war crimes.

Norac, the first general of the Croatian army accused of war crimes, was considered to be a hero of the defense of Gospić. When he disappeared, the whole country went into a state of fervor. Public opinion was polarized: some thought he had done the right thing because it was a disgrace to extradite "our boys" to the tribunal in The Hague; others took the more legalistic angle, that is, even if they were against delivering their fellow Croatians to the tribunal, they were aware that Croatia must meet its international obligations. This uproar lasted for about two weeks, during which time the entire country was held hostage by the Norac case. The socialist government (actually a coalition of six parties dominated by the socialists) was also polarized on how to deal with the problem. In the end, Prime Minister Ivica Račan persuaded Norac to surrender to the police.

But before Norac surrendered, the entire government nearly collapsed. Right-wing parties, especially the HDZ, were hoping for just this; elections would follow and give them, so they believed, a chance to grab power again. The prime minister managed to save his government from the dangerous situation, but that the veterans' demonstrations could produce a crisis of such magnitude made him aware of the kind of power he was dealing with. Especially because the veterans' political protests also turned into something else: the veterans were joined by poor and unemployed people unhappy that the government was not fulfilling its promises, thus turning the meeting into a potentially explosive social uprising.

The result of the uproar over the Norac case was that enormous pressure was exerted on the government and the judges. In addition to the demonstrations, the war veterans threatened to block roads and stop traffic, actions that would destroy the tourist season. Some police and military units openly refused to carry out orders. Then many parliamentarians raised their voices against the arrest of the suspected war criminals. Indeed, three right-wing parties demanded that the parliament rule that Norac could not be arrested. This would be overriding a court decision, an example of direct pressure on the law. The veterans began to stage their demonstrations in front of the court building in Rijeka, holding banners with threatening slogans. The judges also received death threats, which, after the death of Milan Levar, had to be taken seriously.

And political pressure has not been the only difficulty facing the court in Rijeka. The biggest problem has been with witnesses, who can be divided into roughly two groups: executioners—those who took part in executions—and victims—those who were imprisoned and saved by chance or who witnessed the disappearance of their loved ones.

Men who participated in the meeting on the evening of October 16 and the executions following it have tried to minimize their own role or show that they were forced by others to shoot. Their memory served them well when they were asked to describe details of the executions. They remembered the time of the day, which car they used, how people from the truck behaved, and so on and so forth. But they experienced a curious loss of memory when it came to naming those who organized the meeting, ordered executions, and shot civilians.

Some of the five accused have claimed that they don't remember taking part in such a meeting or any executions, no matter that other participants confirmed that they were there. Some, both accused and witnesses, have changed their statements. In his first statement, one of the witnesses, Siniša Glušac, said that he was ordered by Mirko Norac to execute Serbian civilians. Two days later Glušac said that he remembered nothing, that his earlier statement was given under the influence of medication. A witness, Fatima Skula, a secretary of Tihomir Orešković, was badly beaten up after she gave an interview to the weekly *Globus* in which she claimed that she saw Serbian civilians being killed in the building with the crisis headquarters. The next time she is asked to remember something, she may well suffer from amnesia. To make the whole trial even more difficult and more absurd, the defense lawyers have said that if there are no corpses, no crime can have been committed!

The pressure on the prosecution witnesses in Rijeka and

their fear of revenge are so great that many witnesses prefer to keep their mouths shut or to lie, even at the risk of being punished for committing perjury or contempt of court. As they see it, any punishment handed out by the court would be nothing compared with the threats they receive from others.

But there are some witnesses who speak, who have lost a husband, a brother, a father, or a mother. They have been told that if they speak, they "will end up the same way as members of their family in 1991," as one witness said, but this has not stopped them; they've already lost too much. They have testified not only about death squads, men with masked faces who picked up people in the middle of the night, but also about the burning and plundering of their houses by Croatian soldiers. Branka Krajnović, who lost both her parents, testified not only that they were taken away and never seen again but also about her neighbors, the husbands of her friends, who placed explosives in Serbian houses. This kind of testimony is even more painful, because only a few men took part in executing civilians while many more destroyed or stole their property.

There is a big difference between being a witness in a court in Rijeka, with veterans demonstrating outside the building and relatives and friends of the accused sitting in the courtroom, and being a witness at the tribunal in The Hague. In Rijeka, witnesses are much more vulnerable to harassment and threats. The atmosphere of fear and hostility sanctions collective amnesia. How can witnesses speak when judges are not only being threatened but also the public itself is not prepared to hear the truth?

Just how strong the antitribunal feelings continue to be can be judged by the fact that Mirko Norac, together with two other former generals wanted by The Hague, was proclaimed an honorary citizen of the Split and Dalmatian region in April 2002; that is, after the investigation of the Gospić group was over and the trial had begun.

According to the ICTY, from fifteen thousand to twenty-five thousand people should be tried for war crimes committed in Croatia and Bosnia. The Hague will take over some two hundred suspects from the highest echelon; the rest are to be tried in local courts. The trial of the Gospić group is supposed to prove that we are capable of doing it ourselves. It is the first experiment of its kind in Croatia. It is supposed to demonstrate that it indeed is possible for a country to judge its own war criminals instead of allowing The Hague to do so and that the Croatian legal system, as well as public opinion, is prepared for the task.

It is easy to agree with those who say that to extradite Croatian war criminals to the tribunal makes us look like a second-rate country, not a state ruled by law; that it makes us look bad, as if we cannot be a democracy and our legal system is incapable of prosecuting its own citizens. It is true that it is humiliating and that judging war criminals at home should force our country to confront itself with some deeply unpleasant truths about the war and, finally, to close this chapter of history.

But what is happening in Croatia during the trials in Rijeka and Split is just the opposite. It is as if we are all deliberately closing our eyes. Thanks to the brave female judge, Ika Šarić, who on March 24, 2003, sentenced Tihomir Orešković to fifteen years in prison, Mirko Norac to twelve years, and Stjepan Grandić to ten (Ivica Rožić and Milan Čanić were acquitted for lack of evidence), there is hope that Croats will be able to face their bloody past. This trial was important for another reason as well. It was the first time that the national doctrine claiming that in a defensive war Croats could not commit war crimes was finally questioned.

CHAPTER 5

Boys Just Had Fun

Dragoljub Kunarac, Radomir Kovač, and Zoran Vuković—Bosnian Serbs from the town of Foča in the Republika Srpska—were the first men in the legal history of Europe to be sentenced for the torture, slavery, outrages upon the dignity, and mass rapes of Bosnian Muslim women as crimes against humanity. On February 22, 2002, at the International Tribunal for the former Yugoslavia (ICTY) in The Hague, they were sentenced to twenty-eight, twenty, and twelve years in prison, respectively. Six months later, on appeal, their sentences were confirmed.

I DON'T REMEMBER her face or even if I saw it at all. It was probably blurred. Many women who testified in the Foča case were protected from the public by a screen, and their faces, and sometimes their voices, were distorted. But I do remember her voice—or the lack of it.

This woman came to the tribunal as a witness in the case of Dragoljub Kunarac, Radomir Kovač, and Zoran Vuković—the Foča case—but when her turn came, she could not speak. She sat facing Kovač, the man who had raped her daughter, imprisoned her, and finally sold her to a Montenegrin soldier for some two hundred German marks. She had last seen her child boarding a bus that was taking people away from Foča. Ten years passed, the war ended, but her daughter never came back. Now the woman looked at Kovač, but the words did not come. As if someone's hand were squeezing her throat. She tried, you could see that she tried very hard to speak, but all she could let out was a tiny sound.

In the courtroom the prosecutor showed her a photo of her daughter (called A.B. in the court) and asked how old she was when the photo was taken. Instead of giving an answer, the mother cried. But it was not really a cry. It sounded as if there were a microphone inside her belly and you could hear the sobs tearing her apart. It didn't last for more than half a minute, that deep, whining sound, that strange howl like that of an animal so wounded that there was no other sound it could make.

The girl A.B. was twelve years old when she was taken prisoner by Kovač, a man in his forties. I remember when my own daughter was twelve. She had barely gotten her period, wore glasses and sneakers, and was not allowed to go to the movies on her own. She was only a child, as at twelve A.B. was a child, too. Kovač was not just a rapist; he was also a child molester. Not that the distinction mattered much to the girl's mother. What probably mattered to her was to see justice done, to see him punished, although there is no punishment severe enough for what he did, and no punishment would bring her daughter back. Perhaps it was also important to her to tell her story after so many years, to get it out, although in the end all she could get out was that odd sound.

To listen to that voice was unbearable. I can't stand a dog

wailing, much less a human being. There is no greater pain in this world than to lose a child. And she had to sit in front of Kovač and talk about it. And the pain overwhelmed her.

Listening to her cry, Kovač clearly was not impressed. He did not move or change the expression on his face. Maybe he did not hear that sound; he looked as though what was going on in the courtroom did not concern him very much. And the contrast between the weeping mother and the indifferent Kovač summed up this trial: from the point of view of the defendants it was a sheer misunderstanding.

Kovač surely did not show any sign of guilt.

He is a tall, slender man with a long face and short hair. He is even a good-looking man, or at least better looking than his two pals from Foča. Except for that expression on his face. That small, cynical smile almost permanently attached to his mouth that made him look cocky, as if he were standing far above this court for some reason known only to him. I couldn't help thinking that it should get him held in contempt of court. Dressed in a dark gray suit, which in his previous life he had probably worn only for weddings and funerals, he leaned back in his chair as though relaxing. Kovač really looks like somebody you can trust to take your daughter to a hospital in his car. And he might have done so, before the war. But this is after the war. You can't trust him. He would rape her, even a child of twelve. Then he would enslave her, together with other girls between fifteen and twenty years of age. Eventually he would sell her to a Montenegrin soldier, and she would never be seen again.

One of the other rapists from Foča, Dragoljub Kunarac, is

a rather short man in his forties with two strong vertical lines marking his deeply sunken cheeks. His face is hard, as if carved out of wood. He looks dried out, the type of skinny but tough man you often find in mountain villages. His dark curly hair is receding on top and looks untidy, as if he doesn't wash it very often. He has big dark eyes. Nothing about him is pleasant, and it is not difficult to imagine him in a camouflage uniform with a gun in his hand. Unlike Kovač, he leaned forward and watched the judges with a frowning forehead and a tense expression on his face.

When you hear what the third man, Zoran Vuković, did—raped young girls, including one who was no older than fifteen—you would like to be able to say that he looks dangerous. But he looks unthreatening, small and weak, especially standing next to Kovač. He has fair hair and grayish skin and looks pasty. He has no chin, and this lack seems to be his main feature. At the beginning of the trial he was wearing a short beard, probably to compensate for the lack of chin. On this February 22, 2001, the day of sentencing, he is shaved clean and his chin seems to disappear into his chubby neck. His face reveals no emotions. Or perhaps he has none? According to the prosecution he seemed to be less cruel than the others, or perhaps they had less proof of his deeds, although one witness described how Vuković told her that he had to kill her uncle. He had to, he said to her, as if asking for her understanding. Vuković, though the oldest of the three men, seemed to prefer to be led by others. But he was no less cruel or sleazy. After raping a fifteen-year-old girl, he told her that he could have been more brutal with her but was not, because he had a daughter the same age.

If you had met any of these three men before the war, you would probably have thought that they were not particularly violent. They were not very different from other men, just three guys who liked to hang out in local bars. Then the war came, and now it is over. Next thing you know, they are in prison. You read in the newspapers about what they did, and you wonder if it is really possible. Can ordinary men behave like that? Your neighbors, perhaps? Your relatives? No, it cannot be. They look so normal. You look for some obvious sign of perversity, some sign that will help you recognize them as criminals.

"They were low-life people who would go around and beg for cigarettes," said one witness about the three men from Foča. "But when the war broke out, as soon as they managed to put their hands on some rifles, they began to feel big and strong. They were only brave with us, women and children." Perhaps this witness is right: perhaps low-life men can easily turn into war criminals. Perhaps the presiding judge, Florence Mumba, was also right when she said, "What the sum of evidence manifestly demonstrates is the effect a criminal personality will have in times of war on helpless members of the civilian population."

But if she is right, there must have been many such "criminal personalities" around to be able to rape tens of thousands of women and to kill more than two hundred thousand people during the war. There would have had to be thousands upon thousands of men committing such acts. Were the majority of them criminal personalities? This is hard to believe. More likely, the war itself turned ordinary men—a driver, a waiter, and a salesman, the three accused were—into criminals because of opportunism, fear, and, not least, belief. Hundreds of thousands had to have believed that they were right in what they were doing. Otherwise, such large numbers of rapes and murders simply cannot be explained—and this is even scarier.

• • •

The trial must have seemed surreal to the three accused men: the courtroom with the glass wall between the court and the public; the lawyers dressed in long black robes; the judges also in black robes, with purple-red collars; the aseptic, formal atmosphere; the foreign languages that all the participants spoke.

In their small town in the mountains they could not have imagined that the world would be interested in what they did, that it would establish a special court and accuse them of rape as a crime against humanity, and that a woman—a black woman! they'd hardly seen one before except on television—would preside over the court. How strange and inexplicable it must be to sit in a prison in some foreign country far up north, a place they had never even thought of visiting, and to be judged by foreigners. Day in and day out they sat there, Kovač, Kunarac, and Vuković, listening to the women speaking up against them. Not one of the men showed any remorse.

The mother of the young girl A.B. was one of some thirty women who took the floor as a witness against the rapists from Foča. They were nameless women, referred to only as FWS-87, FWS-191, FWS-50, or by their initials. A court usher would roll down a plastic yellow curtain over a part of the glass wall separating the public from the court. On a TV screen in the courtroom, their faces would be obscured and their voices were distorted so that they sounded mechanic, almost metallic. But the defendants could see them, face to face.

The three rapists from Foča probably never imagined that their victims would confront them in a courtroom. They knew that women don't speak about their "shame," especially not Muslim women. This time they were wrong. Raped Bosnian women decided not only to speak up but to do so in front of the International Criminal Tribunal. Often they cried, but they managed to describe precisely how they were taken first to a motel, Buk Bijela, then to the Foča high school and the Partizan hall, and from there to private apartments, where they were turned into slaves and sexually abused for months on end.

Sometimes they were forced to "entertain" Kovač and his pals before being raped by them. The witness FWS-87 recalled several incidents when she and other girls had to strip and dance naked on a table at gunpoint. At other times they were raped to the sweet sound of classical music. "It was so humiliating because I felt as if I was owned by him," FWS-87 said. One girl said that she was forced with a knife at her throat to walk naked through the streets of Foča and down to the river. Some girls were beaten; others were lent, rented, or sold to other soldiers; some disappeared. One said that she was raped by twenty soldiers on the first day, the same day her mother was killed. And for certain sexual offenses, witnesses didn't even have the words to describe them to the court.

There are many men just like the trio from Foča, a small town in the Bosnian mountains, who did the same things they did. It is likely that many of them will never be captured. The Bosnian government estimates that sixty thousand women were raped. The rape of Bosnian women was an instrument of terror against the Muslim population, part of the attempt to ethnically cleanse Bosnia; and the court recognized it as such during the trial. Very few Muslims now live in Foča, renamed Srbinje and today part of Republika Srpska.

The rule of the International Tribunal in The Hague is that every prisoner, when brought before the judges for the first time, has to plead either guilty or not guilty. With only a few exceptions, all of the war criminals brought to the court have pleaded not guilty. Kunarac was one of them, first pleading guilty; but then he changed his mind.

In the case of these three rapists, you really wonder what they mean when they say that they are not guilty. Those who killed or ordered killings can say that they had to do so in order not to be killed themselves, and we can see this as an explanation, although not a justification, of their deeds, of why they would plead not guilty. But the soldiers were not ordered to rape, just generally encouraged to do so because it is an efficient way to frighten and humiliate people, which certainly was the aim of the Republika Srpska armed forces in Bosnia. When the defendants say they are not guilty, do they think that the prosecution won't be able to prove their guilt, or are they convinced that there is nothing to feel guilty about? After all, even if they were a bit rough with girls, they did not kill them, nor did they order them to be killed, as others on trial in that very same courtroom did. For example, compared with the crimes of someone like Goran Jelisić, who actually killed people with his own hands, the crimes committed by the trio from Foča do not even look like crimes, at least not in their own eyes. In their part of the world men often treat their wives like nothing more than cattle. The man is the boss, the woman should shut up and obey him; and it is not unusual for a man to beat up his wife in order to remind her of that. Rape? What is rape? To take a woman whenever and wherever you want? It is a man's right, for sure, as far as his wife is concerned. For raping other women, one could get up to fifteen years in prison, but at home most of those sentenced get away with just one to two years. Compared with murder, rape is nothing, not a big deal anyway. With these girls, the three men from Foča just wanted to have a little fun. Sometimes they were drunk and did not know what they were doing. Sometimes they tested their power over the girls. But they did not mean to harm them.

When the witness FWS-50 was asked how she felt after having been gang-raped, she answered, "I felt dead." But she was not dead, and if you asked Kunarac, Kovač, and Vuković, they would probably say that she ought to be grateful to them for that. They had power; they could have killed the girls. Or others could have killed them. After all, these girls were their prisoners. Kovač even claimed that by keeping the girls in his apartment, he saved their lives. Compared with the mass executions going on around them every day, rape was a harmless little game. These girls were lucky to stay alive, they thought.

Lucky? I have met raped women. I have talked to them. I especially remember one woman from Kozarac, the mother of two children. She had recently come from the Omarska camp. When I greeted her she did not look at me, not into my eyes. She had lost that habit in the camp. In her quick glances I recognized fear. She held her head bent slightly forward, as if expecting a blow at any moment. She knew some of her rapists in the camp by name—they were from a neighboring village—but this did not help her. She described the feeling of humiliation, of absolute helplessness, of a kind of absence from her own body; she told of her desire to disappear, to die instantly. The rape left her feeling dirty, she said, as though she had been wrapped up in a layer of filth like a blanket. She scrubbed herself meticulously over and over, but the feeling did not go away for a long time. She imposed a quarantine on herself: she did not allow her children to touch her, afraid that she would dirty them as well. She was alive, yes. But she did not consider herself lucky.

The presiding judge, Florence Mumba, was a black woman from Zambia with a beautiful, serene face and traditionally plaited hair. When the three rapists from Foča heard that she had been appointed to try their case, they must have been convinced of their bad luck. What could a rapist expect from a female judge? Of course she would be hard on them, of course she would go for the maximum sentence. Besides, she was not even from Europe, so what could she know about that war? She might think that the three of them saw only an opportunity to please themselves; she could not understand that Serbs and Muslims were enemies and that therefore to dishonor Muslim women was, well, somehow legitimate. Everybody was doing it. In their own country, Republika Srpska, they were treated like heroes. Who would arrest them? Who would volunteer to be a witness against them? Their victims came as witnesses to The Hague, yes, but they would not dare to do the same in Foča or Sarajevo or anywhere else in Bosnia, for that matter. They would be afraid that their own people would recognize them.

If it were not for The Hague, Kunarac, Kovač, and Vuković would still be sitting in a café in Foča's main street, smoking, drinking brandy, and telling anecdotes of the war. They would be met with the respect that war veterans get there. And if by accident one of the women they raped happened to pass by, they would point at her—and laugh.

• • •

On February 22, 2001, Judge Florence Mumba asked the three defendants to stand up. She was ready to pass sentence, but first she would explain to each of them why they were being sentenced to make sure that they really understood. Addressing the courtroom, she said, "The three accused are not ordinary soldiers whose morals were merely loosened by the hardships of war. These are men with no known criminal past. However, they thrived in the dark atmosphere of the dehumanization of those believed to be enemies, when one would not even ask, in the words of Eleanor Roosevelt, 'Where, after all, do universal human rights begin? In small places, close to home.' Political leaders and war generals are powerless if the ordinary people refuse to carry out criminal activities in the course of war. Lawless opportunists should expect no mercy, no matter how low their position in the chain of command may be."

Dragoljub Kunarac was the first to be sentenced. He stood and listened carefully to Judge Mumba's words. It was not a long speech, but it was too long for someone waiting to be sentenced. Then she finally turned to him. After listing his crimes, she concluded, "By the totality of these acts you have shown the most glaring disrespect for the women's dignity and their fundamental human right to sexual self-determination, on a scale that far surpasses even what one might call, for lack of a better expression, the 'average seriousness of rapes during wartime.' You abused and ravaged Muslim women because of their ethnicity, and from among their number, you picked whomsoever you fancied on a given occasion. . . . You not only mistreated women and girls yourself but you also organized their transfer to other places, where, as you were fully aware, they would be raped and abused by other soldiers. This behavior calls for a severe penalty commensurate with the gravity of your crimes. The

Trial Chamber therefore sentences you, Dragoljub Kunarac, to a single sentence of twenty-eight years imprisonment. The sentence shall run from today. The time you have spent in custody shall be credited towards the sentence. You may sit down."

There was a brief moment, a few seconds, before Judge Mumba's words were translated into Kunarac's language when hope was still visible on his face. Then he understood and bent his head as if something had hit him. He probably expected a lighter punishment because he had turned himself in, cooperated with the prosecution, and even said that he was sorry for the one rape that he admitted. Now, suddenly, he must have realized that he would be almost seventy when he got out of prison, and I could tell that he didn't quite believe that he had been given such a sentence.

Radomir Kovač's expression didn't change a bit when his turn came. While Judge Mumba enumerated his crimes, he listened with the same idiotic little smile, looking as if he had nothing to do with them, as if he were in the courtroom by sheer accident. But the judge, if she noticed at all, was not bothered by it, and in her calm voice she told him, "Particularly appalling and deplorable is your treatment of the twelve-year-old A.B., a helpless little child for whom you showed absolutely no compassion whatsoever but whom you abused sexually in the same way as the other girls. You finally sold her like an object, in the knowledge that this would almost certainly mean further sexual assaults by other men. . . . The treatment of her is the most striking example of your morally depraved and corrupt character. . . . You relish the absolute power you exerted over their lives, which you made abundantly clear by making them dance naked on a table while you watched." When Kovač heard that he was sentenced to twenty years in prison, he did not even blink.

The third accused, Zoran Vuković, must by now have been aware that his sentence wouldn't be light, either. He too was charged with torture and rape; but for his crimes he got only twelve years because, as it was explained, only one of the incidents underlying those charges had been proven. "The Trial Chamber regards it as a serious matter that you showed a total lack of remorse and moral stature by talking about your own daughter after having raped Witness FWS-50, who was in addition only fifteen years old at the time, and mocked her grief by saying that you could have treated her much worse still," Judge Mumba said, taking a long look at all three men, as if she wanted to be certain that they understood her and understood her well.

Nevertheless, for the three defendants this trial was a misunderstanding. In spite of the long sessions, the many witnesses, and Judge Mumba's excellent speech, none of them fully grasped why he was being punished. The words they had just heard from the judge were too abstract for them, empty words from someone who did not comprehend their situation, they believed. The girls were alive, were they not? Otherwise, how could they have come to The Hague and been witnesses against the three of them? Even the girl A.B. might still be alive somewhere in Montenegro.

They heard their sentences and were visibly devastated by

the "injustice" done to them. Twenty-eight years, twenty years, twelve years for rape, while real murderers were getting much less in the same court? Was that justice? There were many other men in Bosnia doing even worse things to women. Why them, why were only the three of them being so severely punished? Looking at these three men, I could tell that they would serve their sentences regretting only that they were stupid enough to be caught or tricked into surrendering.

CHAPTER 6

He Would Never Hurt a Fly

Goran Jelisić, a Bosnian Serb born in Bijeljina, was sentenced to forty years in prison for executing thirteen prisoners in May 1992 in a Brčko police station and at the Luka prison camp near Brčko. It seems that he actually executed many more than a hundred of them. Most of the prisoners were Muslims.

GORAN JELISIĆ looks like a man you can trust. This young man of thirty, something about his clear, serene face, lively eyes, and big reassuring grin, would make you feel safe sitting next to him in a train compartment at night. A man with such a face usually helps elderly women cross a street, he will stand up in a streetcar to let an invalid sit down, or he will allow you to go ahead of him in a supermarket line. He will return a lost wallet to its owner. Jelisić looks like your best friend, your trusted neighbor, your ideal son-in-law. If he had been a salesman, he would surely have had great success with that innocent face of his.

But he is not innocent.

We tend to believe that good-looking people are good, as we tend to see ugly people as mean. It doesn't have much to

66

do with reality, of course. But I had never seen such a compellingly naïve, boyish face belonging to a killer, and I must say that I was overcome with surprise.

Goran Jelisić was born in 1968, which makes him the same age as my daughter. They belong to the same generation. They could have gone to the same school. They could have been friends. I can imagine him sitting in my kitchen on a winter afternoon with a cup of tea, bent over a textbook, with my daughter explaining to him their history homework (he was not a good pupil and left high school after the first year). I can imagine the two of them going to the movies or a disco club together. I would not have objected to that; he has such a sweet face. I have seen many young men like him pass through my kitchen, confused, not interested in school, but otherwise well behaved and pleasant. Because Jelisić lived in Bijeljina, he probably did not travel abroad very much or speak any foreign languages and hardly listened to the latest music. Nevertheless, he was of the same generation as my daughter and her friends.

Their generation grew up healthy. There was no formula milk and no baby food yet, so we mothers had to cook soup for them and prepare spinach and carrots and fruit juices. There were no Pampers then, either, and cotton diapers are very unpleasant when they are soaked, so they quickly learned to ask for the potty. As children they played outside, in the yards, in parks, on sidewalks in front of houses. There was no danger, at least none that we were aware of at that time.

As they grew older, they were convinced that they were

not different from their peers in the West, because they listened to U2 and Madonna, watched American movies and TV shows, read J.R.R. Tolkien, and wore jeans, just as if it were perfectly normal in Yugoslavia. For my generation, living in a Communist country, jeans were a product of the Western bourgeois society and a sign of decadence; my father would never have allowed me to wear them. But communism meant little to my daughter's generation, and Tito even less. They were young children when he died in 1980 and hardly remembered him at all. They were not marked by the cult of Tito as much as we were. My generation had a strong collective identity. We had grown up solemnly celebrating Tito's birthday—the Day of Youth—on May 25 every year at school, celebrating what we believed he meant for Yugoslavia. We were educated as his children, his pioneers.

In a way, the children of the late sixties are the first "normal" generation. Their grandparents fought in World War II. Their parents grew up in poverty. They grew up in a time of security and abundance. I had to eat all the food on the plate, but my daughter did not. War for them was something they learned about in history class or saw in movies. It had happened more than twenty years before they were even born, and it was not quite real. For my generation, the war was much closer. Even if our parents did not speak about it, we knew that they still lived with the traumas of war. I hated the Germans for what they did to my father; my daughter's generation was indifferent to them.

Their generation was apolitical, too. They learned that politics was for grown-ups. The older generations kept them out of politics on purpose, as we had been, as well. And it looked as though communism would never die, so why bother getting involved? They were not brought up as a rebellious generation. This is because we, their parents, were true believers. We believed what we were told, that "socialism with a human face" was possible, and we did not think that a democratic alternative had to be created. When communism collapsed, we found ourselves without political leaders equipped with democratic ideas. But this vacuum was soon filled with nationalist leaders or with Communists already in power, like Slobodan Milošević, who turned nationalist because it was an easy way to stay in power.

Our children believed that we, their parents, would sort out the political mess. But we did not. When the war broke out, they did not understand that they, born in the late sixties or early seventies, were expected to fight in it. But who else could? This was a paradox: this generation, in a way, had to fight the war of their grandparents. The price was high: many of them were killed, wounded, or turned into invalids; many others fled the country.

• • •

Goran Jelisić loved fishing.

He liked dancing with girls and drinking beer with his pals, but most of all he liked fishing. He could hang out by the river day after day. He had several favorite spots that only he knew about, and when he wanted to fish alone he would go there. Not that he did not like company; on the contrary, he enjoyed competitions and being part of a fishing team. But sometimes he preferred to be alone. His friends from the fishing club would only talk about politics and drink beer, would pay no attention to their fishing rods. For Goran, fishing was a time-out from his daily life. This was the best thing about fishing: you could forget about the world, forget even about yourself, and concentrate on the water surface and the thin nylon thread. It was almost as if you didn't exist, as if you were a tree or a leaf or a blade of grass. Goran enjoyed the feeling when nothing really matters, when who you are is not important, because the river doesn't care about it, nor do the fish.

There was not much to forget, though, at least not before the war. He was aware that his life was just plain and common and that he was not particularly good at anything, except maybe at fishing.

Goran was a good fisherman, and he was not stingy. He often gave fish away to friends or neighbors, to a man in whose house he later stayed after he left the Luka prison camp. He fished for the pleasure of it, but no one could say that Goran was fishing only for himself. He knew places with more fish and places with fewer fish, so choosing one was very important; the rest, of course, was luck.

It was always peaceful at the river. There was something about being alone in nature, a feeling that you were the only man alive. Nobody telling you what to do. You could be your own master. Once Jelisić fell asleep in the grass. When he opened his eyes, he did not know where he was. He did not feel his own body. All he saw was a deep blue sky. He became scared. For a split second it occurred to him that he might be dead. Perhaps this is how one feels when one is dead, a kind of a total absence, he thought. Then he came back, knew that he was alive, glad that he was catching fish. One time somebody—a woman, of course—asked him if he felt sorry for the fish. Sorry? What an amazing thought; it never occurred to him that he could feel anything for the fish. It is the law of nature that rules, and fish are lower beings, he told her. If not, they would be catching us.

One has to be a very patient person to be able to fish for a whole day. Fishing is not a sport for nervous, aggressive people. In his love of fishing, Jelisić reminds me of my son-in-law, who also loves fishing more than a soccer game or the movies. He carefully prepares for it, selecting rods, hooks, bait, bucket, nets. While he is getting ready, he is very excited. Then he sits by the sea without saying a word for hours, totally focused, oblivious to the world. He looks like a Buddhist monk in a kind of a meditative trance. Fishing makes him relaxed and happy.

But it is not quite the innocent sport it seems. Fish have to be killed. Like all fishermen, Jelisić must love the moment when he pulls the line and feels that he has caught a fish. The fish appears from the water, wriggling helplessly on the hook. I can imagine his unhooking the fish and throwing it on the grass. Then watching it gasp for air. But perhaps it isn't like that at all. There are other ways of dealing with fish. If he catches a big fish, a fisherman will usually put a thumb into its mouth and break its neck, making an unpleasant, snapping sound. Or he may throw it in a bucket of water and postpone its end. Maybe Goran is gentle: maybe this is what he does with his fish.

If someone had asked him how he would like to spend his life, Goran would not have hesitated much before giving his answer. But nobody ever asked him what he wanted, and he knew that life was not about fishing. To him, perhaps, it seemed as though people were the fish, big or small, catching and eating each other, and he did not want to be eaten.

Later—after he had left Luka—he would come to the river and just lie there, wishing that it was spring again and that nothing had happened. Sometimes it worked.

One of the witnesses for the defense was the president of the local fishing club. This man could not accept what Jelisić did in Brčko. It did not match up with the image of him as a fisherman. The way he knew Jelisić—sitting on a bank of the Sava River, staring at the water or just sunbathing while occasionally looking at the rod and waiting for a fish to bite— this had nothing to do with the brutality described at the tribunal. He vouched that Jelisić was a nice and quiet man, somebody who for sure would never hurt a fly, let alone people. He said so many nice things about Jelisić that one of the judges angrily reproached him, saying that his moral principles came second to friendship and fishing expeditions. But the man was not impressed. "It is my job to have a professional attitude toward all fishermen," he said.

Goran Jelisić grew up in a working-class family in the small town of Bijeljina, which was about 40 percent Muslim. His mother worked, so he was raised by his grandmother. He grew up on a street where Serbs and Muslims lived together, and many friends of his family were Muslims. They played together, went together to school, to bars, to soccer games.

He did not pay any attention to their Muslim nationality, nor did they to his Serbian one. He was never heard to utter an offensive word about anyone. His neighbors say that he was well brought up and well behaved. He was a good and loyal friend. In the late eighties he did not take Serbian nationalism seriously. He did not pay much attention to the idea that Serbs should all live in one state, and, anyway, politics was for politicians. It had nothing to do with his life, with his friends and fishing. But he turned out to be wrong.

When he finished school, Goran got a job as a farm mechanic. It was not a good job, but at least it was a job at a time when most of his friends were unemployed. He was not pleased about making so little money. If only he had money, he could do something with his life, be independent, start a small business, perhaps even leave Bijeljina, although he would miss it. He had an idea how to make money: by forging checks. He was caught and sentenced to a year and a half in prison.

Jelisić appeared as a character witness for Esad Landjo in the Ćelebići case. He explained at length to the judges how good a person Esad Landjo was and how he helped other prisoners in the Scheveningen prison by, for example, teaching them how to work with a computer, cooking for them, or advising them on how to behave in prison. In fact, Landjo (a Muslim) was another war criminal; his alleged specialty was setting Serbian war prisoners on fire. Jelisić's voice was pleasant, and nothing about him suggested that he himself might become one of the accused.

Even now, in a courtroom, I cannot help seeing Goran as

one of my daughter's generation. Nothing in his life prepared him for war. He served several months in prison for
the check fraud in Bosnia, and when he got out in February
1992, it was because Republika Srpska was releasing prisoners
to provide volunteers for the war. Jelisić volunteered for the
police and in May was sent to a Brčko police station. This was
the beginning of his downfall. I think he became a volunteer
policeman not because he was eager to kill and had long sup-
pressed the desire but because it was hard to avoid becoming
one. Perhaps he did not even know what being a volunteer
actually meant. Once he was there, in that Brčko police station, it was another matter.

Of course, if someone had testified that he had found joy
in seeing fish suffer, it would be at least a small sign that
Jelisić had a bad character long before he ended up beating
and killing prisoners. But his fishing friends said nothing of
the sort. There was, in fact, nothing pathological about his
life and behavior before the war. The image of him drawn by
the witnesses for his defense makes you wonder if they are
really describing the person on trial for murder.

According to them, Jelisić was a good and faithful friend,
ready to take risks in order to help people. The tribunal
found itself caught up in a very peculiar situation: as the defense lawyer pointed out, never before had there been a case
where so many people from a victimized ethnic group acted
as witnesses on behalf of a Serbian defendant.

The people who came to defend him, his neighbors, friends,
and schoolmates—many of them Muslims, including the
president of the fishermen's club—all said that they could

not believe that he had committed those murders, even those who were aware that he had admitted to it. They knew Jelisić as a different man, as a fisherman.

He was quiet and shy, one witness said, and he was known to help everybody: he helped at least seven or eight families in a single street during the war. Another witness remembered how Jelisić helped an old Muslim woman whose windows broke when a bomb exploded in her yard by paying for the repairs. A good friend of many years, also a Muslim, told the judges what Jelisić did for him and his family during and after the war. Not only did Jelisić give money to his wife while the friend was in captivity; he also later helped them cross the border to Serbia so they could flee abroad. Jelisić also helped his friend's sister and her husband to escape in the same way after the war. When the warlord Željko Ražnatović Arkan's paramilitary threatened to kill another of his Muslim friends in their hometown of Bijeljina, Jelisić saved him and his wife, and his mother even spent a few days in Jelisić's house with his parents. And he saved the life of his friend's son when he needed an emergency spleen operation: it was Jelisić who took him to the hospital and covered all the expenses. Another person described him as a "nice and honest boy," and a female friend said that he was "a very well brought up child, on the streets, at school, at home. His behavior was always good."

Why, then, did this nice fisherman end up executing Muslim prisoners?

I have two photos in front of me, two very famous photos that were published all over the world. They are photos of a uniformed man executing a prisoner. They are comparable to the brutal photo from the Vietnam war that shows the Saigon police chief shooting a Vietcong soldier in the head at close range. The only difference seems to be that this execution took place in Bosnia some thirty years later, on May 7, 1992. The executioner is dressed in a police uniform, and his back is turned to the photographer. He is aiming his pistol at the head of a prisoner who is walking about a meter in front of him, his head bent down, aware that he might get a bullet at any moment. In the next photo the prisoner has been shot in the back of his head. At the tribunal, Jelisić confirmed that it was he doing the shooting.

But what exactly happened in his mind before that, before Jelisić raised his arm and fired the bullet that decided not only the future of the prisoner in the photo but his own as well? For after that shot, there was no way back for Jelisić. On that day in May, he started out on a road that six years later brought him to the tribunal in The Hague. What happens to a human being that makes him kill another human being in cold blood? Jelisić killed randomly, whimsically; and he seems to have enjoyed it. According to the prosecution, he acted like the willing executioner. Without such enthusiasts, ethnic cleansing would not be possible, said the prosecutor. But neither the prosecution nor the defense could offer the smallest clue about how he had become an executioner.

Jelisić was twenty-three years old when he executed the prisoner in the photo. Could Jelisić's face lie so much? I wondered, looking at this young man in the courtroom. Nothing, really nothing about him, gave away a violent nature, neither his looks nor his manners, not even the way he expressed himself. Or perhaps . . . well, he had a habit of shaking one leg nervously under the desk while sitting in the courtroom with a perfectly calm expression on his face. He would shake it constantly, all the time. Was this a sign of pathology? What was his true nature? Perhaps being a fisherman was in fact closer to his true nature? While he was in the Scheveningen prison awaiting trial, two psychiatrists were called in to evaluate him. Their report suggested that he was an antisocial personality, narcissistic, immature, and longing for recognition. In their opinion, this made him a borderline personality—bordering on perversity, that is. The psychiatrists, Dr. Van den Bussche and Dr. Duits, used words like "repugnant," "bestial," and "sadistic nature" to describe his behavior toward the prisoners at the Luka camp. The judges sentencing him concluded, in their final words, that he was indeed a disturbed personality.

Surviving prisoners who came to The Hague as witnesses did not use as strong words as the psychiatrists' or offer pronouncements on the character of Goran Jelisić. But several of them described his eyes: "He had very high cheekbones too, and his eyes were somehow unnaturally expressive, like turbid water," one witness said. "He seemed to have been using some stimulants or something like that. Whoever met his eyes, I think, would avoid looking at him again. I think he installed [sic] a kind of fear with his look, especially after he had introduced himself. I don't really know how to put it. . . . I mean our fear, which was already very great, I think, tripled after the look we received from him. That is perhaps how I could put it best." Another man, the witness F, described Jelisić's look as powerful and cruel. His eyes did not laugh, only his mouth. "I used to see that kind of thing in films," F said.

"Hitler was the first Adolf, I am the second," Jelisić used to introduce himself to prisoners. In the Luka camp near Brčko, they trembled on hearing his voice, because it quite literally meant death. He would enter the hangar where the prisoners were kept and pick out victims at random, just by saying "you, you, and you." No names were called out, no accusations or verdicts mentioned. First he would collect the prisoners' money, watches, and jewelry. Often he beat them. This he would do in front of his girlfriend, Monika, who sometimes visited the camp because her brother was in charge of it. Then the prisoners were forced to come out of the hangar, one by one. Jelisić would ask a man to kneel down and place his head over a metal drainage grating. Then he would execute him with two bullets in the back of the head from his pistol, which was equipped with a silencer. For a minute or two before the execution, the man he had chosen would plead for his life: "Don't do this to me. Why me? I haven't done anything." It would not help him. Before killing him, Jelisić would curse his Muslim mother. Indeed, the more fear the victim showed, the more pleasure Jelisić would show in killing him. Afterward, two prisoners would carry the body to a refrigerator truck used to take bodies to a mass grave. Then Jelisić would order the blood cleaned from the grating. Jelisić hated untidiness.

When he was in a good mood, Jelisić would explain how nice it was to kill. "I can see that you are scared. It is nice to kill people this way. I kill them nicely. I don't feel anything." Prisoners from Luka who were witnesses at the tribunal remember how he killed a tall, strong prisoner, a Croat. He first cut off the man's ear. Then he walked him back to the hangar for others to see him. Holding his own ear in his hand, the man pleaded with the prisoners to kill him and not give Jelisić that pleasure. Jelisić took his pistol out and offered it to the prisoners, urging them to kill the man. But nobody volunteered. Jelisić sneered at them, telling them they were not worthy of being allowed to live. In the end, he executed the tall Croat at the grate, the same way he did the others.

Merely by pointing his finger, he decided whether someone lived or died. He executed old men as well as young ones. He killed an eighteen-year-old Muslim girl. He killed an old man because he dropped a bottle of water and a young man because he was married to a Serbian woman. And he kept repeating his score loudly: sixty-eight, seventy-nine, eighty-three . . . Allegedly, he single-handedly executed more than a hundred prisoners in eighteen days in May 1992. He bragged that he had to kill twenty to thirty people before he took his morning coffee. He was sentenced because his killing of thirteen of them was proved.

• • •

Jelisić might have been a nice guy to his friends and neighbors, and he was surely a good fisherman. But he was also a killer, as he himself admitted. He was one of three people accused of war crimes who admitted their crimes in front of the tribunal. He said "I am guilty" on thirty-one counts and yet did not show any real remorse (and just thirteen were actually proved). Although the majority of people he murdered were Muslims, the judges concluded that there was not enough evidence to find Jelisić guilty of genocide; that is, for having had the systematic, conscious intention to wipe Muslims out completely. They claimed that because of the perverse features of his character, Jelisić would probably have willingly killed members of any ethnic group. Therefore the charge of genocide was dropped, and Jelisić was sentenced to forty years in prison for violations of the laws or customs of war as well as for crimes against humanity.

The defense correctly pointed out that Jelisić acted as an executioner only during those eighteen days in May, not before and not after. How was it possible, his lawyers asked, that this man turned into a monster *for only eighteen days*? According to them, the only rational explanation was that he was acting under pressure, that he was killing on command. He was obeying orders and was afraid for his life.

Indeed, this could have been the case. It would fit well with his love of fishing and the calm, benevolent disposition that he usually displayed. But since there was not enough evidence to sustain the claim that he obeyed orders, the tribunal ruled that the opposite was the case and that Jelisić executed prisoners of his own free will.

However, there was more than enough evidence of something else. Several prisoners said that Jelisić obviously enjoyed executing people: he showed off by keeping count, he explained his methods, he explicitly stated that he liked what he was doing. These witnesses also said that the more a man would plead for his life, the more pleasure Jelisić would take in executing him. Evidently it was not the act of killing itself that he liked: killing is a messy business, and Jelisić hated messiness; he was obsessed with cleanliness. Every time he executed a person, the grate had to be cleaned immediately.

What did happen, then, during those eighteen crucial days? Nobody could explain for sure, not even Jelisić himself.

Perhaps what had changed was not the person but the circumstances. There was no longer peace; now there was war. Jelisić could no longer find the opportunity to lie in the grass while the river gently murmured and the world around him stood still. The war changed it all. My son-in-law, too, had to leave behind fishing in his beloved Adriatic Sea when he left for Canada at about the same time Goran Jelisić left for Brčko. The war changed both their lives, but in very different ways. How much of that change was due to a conscious decision, how much to coincidence? Why did one leave for Canada, the other for Brčko? Could it have been the other way around? Could my son-in-law have become a volunteer in the Croatian police instead? I believe that he could not. But why couldn't he, while Jelisić could? I don't know the answer. There are many people who seem to be perfectly normal, but under certain conditions, like those prevailing during war, their pathological side comes forward and dominates their behavior. Could it be that Jelisić always had a pathological side that surfaced only when the conditions permitted?

For the first time in his short life, Goran Jelisić was in a position of power. A little man from Bijeljina, a farm mechanic just out of prison, a fisherman, a nobody—he suddenly had absolute power. He was given a pistol and the freedom to use it, and he became intoxicated by the new possibilities. People said he looked and behaved as if he were on drugs. His eyes were strange, and he was agitated, nervous. And indeed, having power over someone else's life and death may be the strongest drug one can take. To the prisoners, he was like a god. He got high on showing off his power by executing prisoners, that nice-looking young man, Goran, from my daughter's generation.

But I keep thinking that even though he became an executioner, in a deeper sense he was himself a victim. Together with his entire generation, Goran Jelisić was cheated. Many of his parents' generation—my generation—embraced the nationalist ideology and did nothing to prevent the war that grew out of it. They were too opportunistic and too frightened not to follow the leaders they had learned to follow. And many of their children paid for their parents' stupidity, sometimes with their lives. Even a killer who may spend the rest of his in prison, like Goran Jelisić.

CHAPTER 7

"Triumph of Evil"

Radislav Krstić, general of the forces of the Republika Srpska and the deputy commander of the Drina Corps, was the first war criminal sentenced for genocide by the tribunal in The Hague. He was sentenced to forty-six years in prison for crimes committed in the UN-safe area of Srebrenica between July 13 and 19, 1995, when more than seven thousand Muslim men were executed and thirty thousand people were forcibly deported. His adjutant major, Dragan Obrenović, is awaiting trial in The Hague.

GENERAL RADISLAV Krstić looked worried as he entered the courtroom, slightly limping; like many, he had personally paid the price of this war, having lost his leg when he stepped on a mine in December 1994. A slim man of fifty dressed in a dark jacket, he had combed his grayish, thinning hair over his nearly bald head, a sign of his vanity.

Seated hunched behind a desk, a worried frown on his forehead, he threw nervous glances at the judges. I got the impression that he felt uneasy in this place, amid lawyers and judges dressed in solemn black and red robes as though for a theatrical performance. But here, unlike in a theater, the action is for real and deadly serious. From the very beginning of his trial, which lasted more than a year, Krstić wore that expression of anxiety on his face. He looked like a trapped man, a weak man, a man full of fear.

As I sat in the courtroom watching him, I remembered a brief scene from a documentary film about the Republika Srpska forces entering Srebrenica in the afternoon hours of July 11, 1995. The scene shows General Ratko Mladić, commander-in-chief of the Serbian forces, ordering his soldiers to take the enclave. General Mladić, Krstić's direct superior, summons him not by his title or by his full name but by his nickname, Krle, as if they were at some private party. "Krle, come here!" Mladić barks, in the same way he would call a waiter or tell a dog to heel. Looking down at the ground in front of him, Krstić follows him, though not very willingly. This short scene, to me, sums up their relationship: that of an aggressive dominating master and his submissive servant. A relationship that Krstić will have to pay for with forty-six years in jail.

In his opening statement, the prosecutor, Mark Harmon, said: "This is a case about the triumph of evil, a story about how officers and soldiers of the Bosnian Serb army—men who professed to be professional soldiers, men who professed to represent the ideals of a distinguished and Serbian past—organized, planned, and willingly participated in genocide or stood silent in the face of it. The authors of these foul deeds have left a legacy that has stained the reputation of the Serbian people and has disgraced the honorable profession of arms."

But this was not so clear-cut when the trial started. My

first impression of Krstić—the way he talked, the tone of his voice, the consideration he showed when he listened to the testimony of victims, and the air of naïveté about him—was not of a man who could have taken part in such horrible deeds as the mass executions of Muslim men from Srebrenica. He looked anxious and frightened, not like a vicious bully poisoned by hatred and hungry for revenge. Even in the documentary film, which showed him dressed in his uniform and standing next to General Mladić in Srebrenica, he didn't strike me as a military man the same way that Mladić did; he didn't look at all like an aggressive person. He seemed too silent, too withdrawn, and too intellectual, more like an army bureaucrat content to shuffle papers at his desk than to lead soldiers into battle. The image he wanted to convey in front of the tribunal was that of a person of integrity, of a professional soldier.

Krstić reminds me of my father, who ended up as a professional soldier right after World War II was over. Becoming an officer in the victorious army of Tito's Partisans was a good career opportunity for him, certainly better than being demobilized and having to go back to his old job as a carpenter. But I always thought of my father as more of a white-collar office man, with an appetite for elegant clothes, good food, and dances at the officers' club, things that would make a real soldier soft. And indeed, at the end of his military career, he was just doing paperwork, and because of his bad health he took early retirement. This is exactly what Krstić would have done if it hadn't been for the war.

My father's uniform always smelled of a mixture of tobacco and vinegar. It was back in the early fifties, and he probably had only one. I remember how my mother would iron it on the kitchen table every Sunday afternoon while my father listened to a soccer game on the radio, his head bent close to the set. Mother would pour water into a metal bowl and add a few drops of red wine vinegar to it. That will freshen up the color, she used to say. Then she would dip a thin piece of cloth into the bowl, wring it out, and smooth it over the trousers laid on the table. She would heat up the heavy black iron on the stove, then press it firmly onto the cloth; each time she did a cloud of steam would rise, hissing, from the table. Father's uniform would always be perfectly ironed, but every time I kissed him I smelled that pungent odor.

Without his uniform, my father was a quite different man, as if he had been deprived of his power. Suddenly he was smaller, somehow weaker and quieter. I thought of this as I watched Krstić sitting there in the courtroom in his dark blue blazer, looking lost. His uniform seemed to have given him his identity, and I even wondered if it had had the same smell as my father's that I could not forget, that reminded me of his different selves. It must have been very humiliating for him to sit there dressed as a simple civilian.

Because he reminded me so much of my father, I had a hard time remembering that Krstić is of my generation, not my father's. When I heard that he had been arrested by UN forces in 1998, I did not even realize this immediately, because I did not know anyone from my generation who had joined the army. It was not a profession that the young men

I knew ever considered. We were city kids, studying fancy subjects like philosophy, art history, or psychology at the philosophical faculty of Zagreb University.

But it was different for someone born in a remote Bosnian village. Becoming a professional soldier might be the only way out of such a village, especially if his parents were poor peasants. A uniform would guarantee a hot meal, proper clothes, a pair of shoes, free lodging, salary, and one fewer mouth for his parents to feed. There is enormous respect for a uniform in any such village. A uniform, any uniform, means power, and power is respected and feared. And even for the supposedly egalitarian Yugoslav society, becoming an officer has always meant a rise in status.

There were many reasons for young Radislav Krstić to become an officer. In addition to getting out into the world, an officer would be decently paid and, if he got married, could get an apartment. This was a big advantage from the point of view of us, his peers. As snobbish as we were, we had to go on living with our parents in their apartment, even after we got married and had babies. Having our own apartment was beyond our dreams. We could not afford to rent one for ourselves. But in spite of their advantages, we all knew that under their uniforms, Krstić and other young men like him were different from us. Under their uniforms they were still country boys, scared and out of place in the city. And although Krstić's wife certainly must have used an electric iron to press his uniform, rather than one she had to heat up on the stove, he seemed to belong both to my father's generation and to mine.

But there were plenty of things that identified him as part of my generation: growing up with the cult of Tito's personality, the glorification of the Partisan struggle against fascism, the Communist revolution during World War II, and, most important, the ruling ideology of brotherhood and unity *(bratstvo i jedinstvo)*, that is, of different nations' living happily together in a common Yugoslavia. In that sense, Krstić's childhood and youth in his small village were probably not so different from mine in the city. In Vlasenica and Han Pijesak, where Krstić went to school, he would have learned from textbooks similar to the ones I had to read. We grew up hearing the same stories, like the one about young Tito preparing a smoked pig's head for his little brothers and sisters (who got diarrhea afterward) and the one about Boško Buha, the young Partisan courier who became a hero. We learned all the Partisan offensives by heart. Sometime in the early sixties Krstić and his class from school probably visited the battle site of Sutjeska at Tjentište or the Ustashe concentration camp in Jasenovac, just as I did with my class. They sang the same patriotic songs we did. Schoolchildren used to watch mandatory movies about the Partisans, about the battles of Neretva and Kozara and the attack on Drvar. Every May 25, the Day of Youth and Tito's birthday, the young Krstić probably sat in front of his TV set watching the celebrations in a sports stadium in Belgrade: the arrival of relay runners in Tito's honor, the spectacular gymnastics display. Later, he and his family probably enjoyed the TV series *Pozorište u kući* (Theater at Home) and laughed at its popular comic actor, Čkalja. They ate *sarma* (minced meat wrapped in sauerkraut) on New Year's Eve. I can even imagine that his first car was a small Fiat 750, nicknamed Fićo, and that he spent his summer holidays in Brela or Makarska on the Adriatic coast.

But neither he nor I ever thought that one day it would be different. Yugoslavia seemed so safe. Brotherhood and unity seemed so real. We grew up together, went to school together—Serbs and Croats and Muslims—befriended each other, got married, had children, never thinking that nationality could be something that would split us apart. The only exceptions were the Albanians. The few who lived in Croatia worked mostly as goldsmiths or in ice cream parlors. In Serbia, they did the dirtiest and most poorly paid jobs. It was difficult to mix with them, not because of the language barrier—most of them spoke Serbo-Croatian—but because of their low social status. We looked upon them as people who came from an altogether different and inferior world.

In his opening remarks at the tribunal, speaking about his life, Krstić confirmed that "... never had there been any incidents, anything that would have been caused by national intolerance. Quite contrary. We all went to school together, we socialized together, and we had a great respect for each other. This applied also to the elderly population of the village, but it applied in particular to the younger generation." I knew what Krstić meant; I could have said the same thing. I remember my school pals from Serbia, Macedonia, and Bosnia, with their strange names and strange dialects. We were aware of the differences, of course, but they did not bother us at all.

Apart from school, the army was one of the government's means of creating brotherhood and unity. Young conscripts were sent far away from home to get acquainted with their country. The Yugoslav National Army (JNA) was considered to be the people's army and "the biggest school of brotherhood and unity," one of the very guarantees of statehood. It is truly a terrible paradox of the war that the same army that had the important role of building brotherhood and unity in the peoples of Yugoslavia turned into the main instrument against it.

The urge to overcome traditional national divisions was revealed in a census held in 1981 in which some 1.2 million people declared themselves to be "Yugoslavs." This group was the sixth largest "nation" in Yugoslavia at that time and consisted mostly of people of the postwar generation, many of them urban professionals and from mixed marriages. This might have been the beginning of a Yugoslav melting pot, except that it did not work. We did not all become Yugoslavs.

When he spoke about his past, especially the nine years he spent in Sarajevo, from 1972 to 1981, General Krstić sounded nostalgic, almost romantic. He got married, had a daughter, and lived in his own apartment. "Those were beautiful years of my life," Krstić said. But there was something about Sarajevo that he especially appreciated, something that other cities in Yugoslavia did not have. "This spirit of unity was particularly pronounced in the town of Sarajevo. We never inquired about each other's ethnic backgrounds. We all felt like residents of Sarajevo," he observed, perhaps forgetting for a moment that he was in a courtroom and that his words might sound unconvincing to the judges and the audience.

In 1991 the war started, first in Slovenia, then in Croatia. The breakup of Yugoslavia was painful and horrible for Krstić, as he acknowledged at the tribunal. Indeed, it must have been distressing for him to see how everything that he believed in went down the drain. In those years I thought a lot about my father—who had died in November 1989—and how the changes would have affected him. I would not have wanted him to see Yugoslavia falling apart because of the nationalism he fought against all his life. I would not have wanted him to see a Partisan general turn into a profascist politician, like Franjo Tudjman, who came into power in Croatia. This must have been confusing and frightening for Krstić: he was not a man of politics, and, as he himself said, he had underestimated the role politics played in bringing the war about.

But Krstić still believed that Bosnia would not succumb to the war. Like the majority of Bosnians, he was convinced that war could not occur in such an ethnically mixed country. Here I would have agreed with him. I was in Sarajevo, too, and I felt the same relaxed, tolerant atmosphere there. Even after the war started in Croatia, people in Sarajevo used to say, "Nobody can divide us. Muslims, Serbs, and Croats live here on the same floor of apartment buildings." There was no history of ethnic clashes over the last forty-five years, and one-third of the children came from mixed marriages. Nevertheless, in April 1992, war came to Bosnia.

That year Krstić was in Priština. Around him officers of non-Serbian background were leaving the Yugoslav National Army Corps. Finally, in the middle of that year, after Bosnia had proclaimed its independence, Krstić understood that it was his turn to choose where he wanted to live, in Serbia or in Bosnia. He decided on Bosnia, where he was born. But when he arrived there, he saw that it had become deeply divided among Serbs, Croats, and Muslims. He was a Serb, and perhaps for the first time he was in the position to fully realize the implications of this. For him, as for so many others, his nationality became his destiny. So in June of that year, with the war already raging, he joined the armed forces of the Republika Srpska.

So far I could follow him: I could see how his life unfolded, and I could understand his disappointments, his confusion, his naïveté, and his fears. I could also understand his trust in politicians; in a Communist country, politicians were the ones who were supposed to solve problems. Krstić was convinced that the politicians must find a solution, and in this he was not alone. People placed so much faith in a political solution that they did not see through a politician like Slobodan Milošević. The country was falling apart, and Milošević's only goal was to stay in power, even if the price was war. Serbian media stirred people into a nationalist fervor, spreading propaganda until Serbs in both Serbia and Bosnia were completely convinced that they were threatened by the "others." The Croatian and Bosnian media soon joined the frenzy. Vukovar was destroyed, Dubrovnik was shelled, Sarajevo was besieged—and still Krstić harbored some naïve hope that there could be a political solution to the Bosnian situation.

As I looked at Krstić in the courtroom, there were moments, I admit, when I felt sorry for him. I thought about what he said and what he did not say, and I especially thought about a question that nobody asked him, although it seems to me the most important one: how was it possible that a person who grew up without ethnic prejudices, a professional officer who was educated in the Yugoslav National Army in the spirit of brotherhood and unity, could end up being accused of genocide of his Muslim neighbors? If he was really so ethnically unbiased, if he enjoyed ethnically mixed Sarajevo so much, why did he support the nationalist politics of Republika Srpska? How did he find himself in a situation of ordering the killing of people whom, only yesterday, he was protecting? How could any person of basic integrity do that?

Perhaps Krstić acted against all his instincts, behaved in a manner contrary to everything that he had ever learned and loved, in effect denied his very self. But this could have cost him his sanity. Perhaps he convinced himself that he had to save his own life and that he should also act in defense of his own people. Once the war started, people had to choose, they had to take sides. Sometimes this meant splitting up a family. Krstić's situation was dramatic, yes, but no more so than anybody else's. If people did not want to take sides, they often had to leave the country. There were many such cases. There were also people of different nationalities who continued living together throughout the war, especially in Sarajevo. But the majority did take sides, and for Krstić, a professional soldier, this meant joining the armed forces of the Republika Srpska.

At this point, at the beginning of the war in Bosnia, this man who loved Sarajevo so much did not choose to return there. Perhaps this was because it was besieged, perhaps it was also because he no longer felt like a Sarajevan. With his peasant background, he preferred a village, where he felt safer. Sarajevans used to say that the war in Bosnia was a war of peasants against city dwellers, with the former led by people like Radovan Karadžić, who was from a small village in Montenegro and understood little of urban life. Such a man never really fit into Sarajevo and felt humiliated by its citizens; now he had his chance to take revenge.

Once Krstić decided to join the Republika Srpska forces, the rest of what happened to him was more or less determined by circumstances. In the next three years he was promoted several times, the last time when he was made lieutenant general and deputy chief of staff of the Drina Corps. A month later, in July 1995, the Drina Corps was given an assignment in the towns of Srebrenica and Žepa. At the same time the chief of staff of the Republika Srpska troops, General Ratko Mladić, took over the command in Srebrenica. For Krstić this was an ominous moment, the moment when his compliant character "allowed" him to choose the wrong side, when he "agreed to evil," as the prosecutor Mark Harmon said. This was the moment when he should have resisted the forces of circumstances, assuming, of course, that Krstić was indeed against the deportation and extermination of Muslims. In fact, Krstić could not resist these forces; he did not have the strength. He was an opportunist who went with the tide. In the three years since he had joined the armed forces of the Republika Srpska, he had come to the point where he could no longer refuse to obey orders from General Mladić. But during his time in Srebrenica, he must at least have been aware of the consequences.

I do not believe that Krstić is a pathological case, an evil man who hated Muslims and wanted to destroy them. But he does strike me as somebody who struggles with himself. He is a weak man, a man who is afraid to say no to a higher authority. This happened to thousands of others, too. This policy of small steps, of everyday decisions and concessions, of a collaboration on a much smaller scale, brought men like Krstić into situations where they had to either obey or oppose the orders issued by men like Ratko Mladić. In Krstić's case, the order was to kill the Muslims from Srebrenica. Krstić could have disobeyed Mladić. He could have resigned or issued a counterorder. Instead, he decided to do nothing. Opposing Mladić would have proven too costly for him, as he tried to explain to the tribunal: "Not in my wildest dreams was I able to undertake any measures. We weren't allowed to talk about anything like that, let alone take steps against a commanding officer, regardless of my knowledge that he or somebody else had perhaps committed a war crime." The only justification for going along that he offered the judges was his own cowardice.

The fact is that Krstić did not object when Mladić took over the command of his troops and started issuing orders;

he remained silent when Mladić threatened to exterminate people in Srebrenica. Krstić claimed that he did not know about the mass executions; still, it seems unlikely that he would have done anything to stop them if he *had* known. Indeed, by the time the executions started, it was too late to do anything. Mladić's authority was too great. An officer does not challenge his superiors, certainly not if he had previously served in the Yugoslav National Army. Every army is, by definition, an authoritarian institution, and a Communist army even more so; and Mladić was not a person one could oppose without fearing the consequences. Radislav Krstić admitted that he was scared of Ratko Mladić, both while they were in Srebrenica and after what happened there. Several times during his cross-examination, Krstić said that he had feared for his family and for himself. The judges, however, seemed unimpressed; in their eyes this was not an excuse. There are such things as rules of war, ethics of war, and an officer's honor, and it was Krstić's duty to respect those values and to prevent war crimes. If he couldn't, he should have reported them. He didn't. Not knowing about the crimes while they were taking place should not have prevented him from reporting them the moment he did find out about them. But to whom? To his superiors, Mladić and Karadžić? Or to UNPROFOR (the United Nations Protection Force)? In all fairness, we do have to stop here and think: what could Krstić have possibly done?

On the other hand, perhaps the idea of individual responsibility was simply too abstract for General Krstić. After all, where would he have learned about it? Communist society, like the nationalist one that replaced it, is a collective society; there is no such thing as individual responsibility because there is very little individualism.

Still, we must ask ourselves: how does our neighbor become our enemy? How do we internalize the enemy, and how long does it take to do so? By the time the enclave of Srebrenica fell, the Serbian propaganda machine, especially television, had been demonizing the enemy—Croats, Bosnian Muslims, and Albanians—for almost ten years. Srebrenica's fall and the mass executions that followed were made possible only by long psychological preparation. By 1995 the Muslims had become a nonpeople, much like the Jews during the Second World War. The extermination of Jews also began with small steps. Little things, such as not being allowed to buy flowers in a local shop, have your hair cut at the hairdresser, or ride a streetcar, eventually led them to the gas chamber.

In Bosnia numerous war crimes had been committed before 1995 by participants on all sides of the conflict, all in the name of the nation. The offensive on the Srebrenica enclave was apparently in retaliation for an earlier attack of the Bosnian Muslim forces on the neighboring Serbian village of Kravice, in which many Serbian civilians were killed. Hence, perhaps, killing Muslims was justified in the eyes of the perpetrators, including those of Krstić himself. But what took place in Srebrenica was not just a military operation—with "collateral damage"—but a deliberate act of ethnic cleansing. In a concerted effort to rid the Drina valley area of its entire Muslim population, more than seven thousand men were summarily executed and thirty thousand women, children, and elderly people were forcibly deported. This was done according to the instructions of the president of the Republika Srpska, Radovan Karadžić, to "create an unbearable situation of total insecurity with no hope of future survival or life for the inhabitants of Srebrenica and Žepa."

Amazingly, there is often at least one person who manages to survive a mass execution. One of them, a witness in the tribunal known as O, took the stand at the Krstić trial to tell about the biggest mass killing in Europe since the Second World War. He was just seventeen years old when it happened: "Some people shouted, 'Give us some water first, then kill us.' I was really sorry that I would die thirsty, and I was trying to hide among the people as long as I could, like everybody else. I just wanted to live for another second or two. And when it was my turn, I jumped out with what I believe were four other people. I was walking with my head bent down, and I wasn't feeling anything. . . . I saw rows of killed people. It looked as if they had been lined up, one row after the other. And then I thought that I would die very fast, that I would not suffer. And I just thought that my mother would never know where I had ended up."

While the young man called Witness O was speaking in the tribunal, Krstić seemed visibly shaken by his words. He did not know where to look. This underscored even more my impression of his compassion for his victims. He appeared to find it almost unbearable to listen to this witness, as if this one young man, who had almost been among the seven thousand murdered, who had survived only by chance to tell about it, finally brought home to Krstić the reality of his deeds. Then the prosecutor started to cross-examine Krstić, and my perception of him changed drastically.

Krstić's line of defense was a simple one. He did not deny that war crimes had been committed by the Republika Srpska units, but he denied issuing orders for these crimes. General Mladić outranked him and always took over the command. Krstić argued that Mladić issued the orders himself directly to the battalion commanders. Day after day in cross-examination, he tried to convince the prosecutor and the judges that he had nothing to do with the entire operation. In other words, Krstić's strategy was complete denial. He denied not only participating in the planning, organizing, and ordering of the killings and deportations but also even knowing that they were happening. Indeed, he declared, he was not even there at the time. Beginning with the afternoon of July 12, he was in Žepa and heard nothing about what was going on in Srebrenica. In fact, he said, he first learned about most of the atrocities at his trial.

He frequently answered the prosecutor's questions with "I don't know," even when it was highly improbable, even when he must have known. For example, as early as July 17, 1995, an adviser to Radovan Karadžić publicly denied accusations that there was torture, killing, and deportation of Muslim civilians in Srebrenica, claiming that they were treated well by the Serbs. Reports in the world press of suspicion that war crimes had been committed in Srebrenica appeared very early, and even the official Chinese news agency had written about them by the seventeenth of July. But no, General Krstić had heard nothing.

When the prosecutor asked him if, while driving toward Potočari, he had seen any of the many buses and trucks that were dispatched to transport people out of the enclave, Krstić said he had not noticed them. These events happened in an area of some forty square kilometers, and Krstić actually gave an interview on camera with a number of parked buses in the background. It was like the deputy mayor of a small town saying he didn't notice a big soccer game going on in his town or the convoy of fifty or sixty buses or the thousands of fans in the streets or the traffic jams and the policemen everywhere . . .

As the prosecutor showed, it was simply impossible for a person in Krstić's position not to notice what was happening around him. Deporting thirty thousand people and killing seven thousand: that was a very big and difficult logistic operation. It required the cooperation, knowledge, and participation of countless soldiers, as the prosecutor, Peter McCloskey, pointed out at the trial: "First, it involved the issuing, the transmitting, and the dissemination of orders to all units that participated in the movement, the killing, the burial, and reburial of the victims. It involved the assembling of a sufficient number of vehicles and buses, trucks, to transport the thousands of victims from the location of their capture and surrender to detention centers that were located near the execution sites. It involved obtaining fuel for these vehicles, providing guards and security for each of the vehicles, identifying detention centers that were secure enough and in close proximity to the execution fields. It involved obtaining sufficient numbers of blindfolds and ligatures so these prisoners could be bound before they were executed; sufficient men to secure the actual detention facilities themselves, to guard the prisoners for the days or for the hours that they were kept there before they were executed; obtaining transportation; organizing the killing squads and arming the killing squads; the requisitioning and transportation of heavy-duty equipment necessary to dig the large mass graves; and it required men to bury the thousands of victims whom we were later to discover." In September of that same year, 1995, the mass graves were dug up, and the bodies were transferred to a variety of distant locations. Even if he was in Žepa, General Krstić was fully aware of what was happening. It was his officers and soldiers from the Drina Corps who participated in this systematic operation, including the cover-up.

At the tribunal Krstić was obviously lying and very unconvincingly. But he didn't seem to be lying in order to receive a reduced sentence, because he already knew that he would be sentenced not only for his individual accountability but also for his responsibility as a commander. More likely he lied in the futile expectation that with all the blame for Srebrenica falling on Mladić, he could save his own face and self-respect. Or there could be another reason. In his mind, his responsibility could be proven only if he was caught with the smoking gun in his hand. Besides, in Bosnia, Serbia, or Croatia, one does not necessarily have to be ashamed of lying. I remember how astonished Western ambassadors, politicians, and envoys usually were after meetings with Mladić, Karadžić or Milošević: looking straight into Lord Owen's, Carl Bildt's, or Richard Holbrooke's eyes, these men would lie, give their word of honor, and sign treaties they didn't intend to uphold without thinking twice. It took some time before Westerners realized that. Life in post-Communist societies—as in Communist ones—is immersed in a culture of lies. There is no moral code that admonishes "Thou Shalt Not Lie!" On the contrary, anyone can see with his own eyes that by lying one survives and profits and that telling the truth is stupid.

If there was ever a chance for Krstić to convince the prosecution, the judges, and the public of the truthfulness of what he said, to make them believe that he was a professional officer and a man of integrity, it was irrevocably lost when McCloskey produced a tape recording of an intercepted conversation between Krstić and his adjutant major, Dragan Obrenović. Before playing the tape, McCloskey asked, "General Krstić, did you ever order the killing of Muslims?" Vehemently, Krstić answered, "No!" Then McCloskey played the tape, and it became clear why he had asked the question.

> *Krstić:* Are you working down there?
> *Obrenović:* Of course we're working.
> *Krstić:* Good.

Obrenović: We've managed to catch a few more, either by gunpoint or in mines [mine fields].

Krstić: Kill them all, Goddamn it!

Obrenović: Everything is going according to plan.

Krstić: Single one must not be left alive.

Obrenović: Everything is going according to plan. Everything.

Krstić: Way to go, chief. The Turks are probably listening to us. Let them listen, the motherfuckers. ["Turks" is a derogatory name for Muslims in Bosnia.]

There was a short pause after the prosecutor played the tape. He looked at Krstić. Everybody looked at him. General Krstić lowered his head and covered his face with his hands. It was a gesture of sheer despair, as though he might start to cry. It must have been clear to him that this was the end of everything, of his hope to finish his trial with his integrity and his officer's honor intact. This was the end, and he knew it. He was devastated. Sitting in the courtroom in the dock, he seemed to have shrunk; he suddenly seemed more vulnerable than ever. Once again, I felt pity for him, because he had miscalculated so badly. He apparently had not counted upon the prosecution's having such damning evidence as that taped conversation.

"General Krstić, did you, on August 2, 1995, tell Major Obrenović to kill the people he captured that day?" the prosecutor asked him. Suddenly, in a dramatic transformation, Krstić almost shouted at him: "No, Mr. McCloskey! This is one hundred percent montage! On that day I didn't talk to Obrenović at all. Second, I did not recognize the other participant in the conversation and especially not my own voice, myself. I repeat: This is a montage, one hundred percent rigged."

It was the only moment during the entire trial when Krstić reacted strongly, almost militantly. It was probably because he was truly scared that he had been caught lying and that his actions had finally caught up with him. After all, Krstić had given the order to kill. He had actually said those words, even if he denied it.

Yet although the taped conversation had been intercepted by two different sources, the court refrained from taking it into consideration when the judges decided upon his sentence; they had enough other evidence.

After Srebrenica, Krstić had apparently signed a document in support of General Mladić in his power struggle with the president, Radovan Karadžić. At that time, Krstić—as he himself admitted—was aware that Mladić had committed war atrocities. "I had to sign it because all other generals signed it; can you imagine what would happen to me if I had not signed it?" he said, his tired voice quivering slightly. It was the end of the day. McCloskey looked at Krstić; by now even he appeared to feel sorry for him. Then he listed the names of five generals who did not sign the document yet were alive and well. He asked Krstić the question that every single person in that courtroom probably wanted to ask him: "Why didn't you just retire, General, when this all happened? Was that the right choice, General? Did you make the right choice?" It was the coup de grâce. General Krstić, crushed and demoralized, could only reply, "I'd rather not answer that question."

Perhaps Krstić was naïve enough to believe that if he had only been skillful enough, he could have tricked the prosecution, convinced them that Mladić was the only culprit. Krstić wanted to portray himself as a bystander. But in war there are no bystanders. In Srebrenica, General Krstić was most definitely not one; he was heavily implicated. Or in the words of one judge, Almiro Rodrigues: "But you were there, General Krstić, you heard, you gave orders, you knew! You were there when they began to separate men from the women, children, and old people. You could not *not* have seen their physical condition. You could not *not* have heard the screams of the men who were taken to the building called the White House as they were being beaten."

The man who had entered the courtroom with an air of naïveté, compliant and ready to please the judges, but one who did not have the guts to confront Mladić, who portrayed himself as a victim of circumstances: this man was at last totally revealed. In his trial was the evidence of the collapse of a society that had lost its values, of an army that had lost its honorable reputation, and of a man who had lost his soul when he agreed to allow evil.

CHAPTER 8

One Day in the Life of Dražen Erdemović

Dražen Erdemović, born in 1971 in Tuzla, Bosnia, of a Croatian mother and a Serbian father, was accused of crimes against humanity for taking part in a massacre of Muslim men from Srebrenica on July 16, 1995. During the investigation and the trial, he repeatedly expressed his remorse for the crimes he had committed. Erdemović explained that he was forced to shoot because when he refused, his commander threatened him with death. His initial sentence was ten years in prison. On appeal it was reduced to five years because the tribunal acknowledged that Erdemović had acted under extreme duress. He was a witness for the prosecution in the Krstić case and in the Karadžić-Mladić case. Today he is free and enjoys the status of a protected witness.

IT WAS already past nine o'clock in the morning when Dražen Erdemović and his unit arrived at the Branjevo collective farm. They had not been told what their task would be. Their commander, Brano Gojković, had not been talkative during the bus ride from their base in Vlasenica; he hadn't even told his soldiers where they were going. Dražen did not like it. Their Tenth Sabotage Detachment of the armed forces of the Republika Srpska usually had clear tasks, like reconnaissance missions or planting explosives in the territory of the enemy, and they were always informed about them well in advance. But this was different. Whatever the mission was, it was secret. The only thing Dražen knew was that they were bringing a lot of ammunition with them, for both pistols and automatic weapons.

It was not a long drive, and when they got out of the bus they found themselves near a farm. It was a pig farm, but it seemed deserted; there were no animals to be seen and no people except a single watchman. There was a big oak tree in the yard, and Dražen and several other soldiers sat under it. Although it was still early in the morning, it was already hot. Dražen looked at the fields surrounding the farm, the nearby woods shimmering in the heat, and the blue mountains beyond. The view was beautiful. It reminded him of the small village where his parents used to live once and where he used to spend his summers as a child with his grandmother. Bosnia was beautiful; he had always thought so. Not that he had traveled enough to be able to make comparisons, but he had heard this from others as well. If only he could go to a river and swim! Yes, that was what he wanted to do. Just as he did when he was a small boy, swimming in the stream near his village with his pals, feasting on a tomato and a piece of bread spread with lard that his grandmother had given him for lunch. Dražen still could remember the feeling when, hot from running, he would jump into the cold water and afterward bite into a tomato warmed by the sun.

But he had not come to Branjevo to swim. He lit a cigarette, somewhat uneasy. What are we waiting for? he asked Ivan, a soldier sitting next to him, a Croat. Ivan was not in a good mood, either. Don't ask too much, he murmured. Dražen decided to let it go and lay down. The grass under the tree was still cool and wet from the morning dew. The sky above was so blue that it hurt his eyes. He closed them and let his thoughts drift. If only he could get out of the whole thing, the war, this uniform of his, the shooting. He had never liked being a soldier and never thought he was a good one. He had never demonstrated any enthusiasm for it and for this reason had not made much of a career in the army. Once he had been promoted, but he held the new rank for only two months before his superiors detected how reluctant a soldier he was. Things never worked out for him; it was almost as if there was an outside force determining his life. He should have stayed in Tuzla, but there was no work there for a locksmith, which was what he was before joining the army. Besides, all the men his age had been drafted into Serbian, Croatian, or Bosnian units. He was drafted by the Yugoslav National Army (JNA) in 1990. He served as an army policeman in Belgrade, then was sent to fight against Croats in Slavonia. He came back to Tuzla in 1992 but was soon mobilized by the Croatian Council of Defense (HVO) units in Herzegovina. After a year he got out of the HVO and for some time tried to avoid the war. Then he got married. Soon a baby was born. Things just seemed to happen to him. Like now. He and his wife had come to Republika Srpska because he had managed to arrange to get documents so that they could leave their country, which had gone mad. But when they arrived in the town of Bijeljina, the man with their documents didn't show up. So they were stuck there, with a small baby boy and no money. Dražen had to find a job. Three months earlier a friend had told him that the armed forces of the Republika Srpska paid well and would provide him with a house too. And indeed, Dražen was soon allotted a house that had belonged to a Muslim, but he considered being a soldier a temporary solution. He was much more concerned with trying to obtain valid documents that would enable him and his young family to leave. This was the easiest way out, or so Dražen thought. But instead of going to Switzerland, he ended up in Branjevo.

At first it was all right; his squad wasn't really involved in actual fighting. He had been a soldier for four years now, in different units and in different parts of what used to be Yugoslavia, but he was still finding this war unreal, as when you are part of something but feel as if you're not really there. That was how Dražen felt: he was there in his uniform, but never fully present.

Lying in the grass now on the Branjevo farm, he felt a slight vibration in the ground. It reminded him of the time he had put his ear on a train track and could hear the locomotive coming long before it appeared from behind a nearby hill. He stood up and looked around. The others were not alerted yet, but soon they would be. A bus was coming toward them. It was a rather battered bus, one of those buses that take peasants between villages and break down more often than not. Dražen could see the name Centrotrans written on it in big letters and a few soldiers sitting in the front. It stopped before the main building, some fifteen yards from them. Their commander briefly spoke to the driver while two other soldiers opened the rear door. A man appeared. Dražen will remember him forever, because at that moment it became clear to him what their task was to be and he suddenly shivered. The man was tall and very thin and had a mustache. Dražen could not tell his age because the man was blindfolded with a piece of dirty cloth. He wore a bluish shirt soaked with sweat, a pair of blue trousers with white stripes down the sides, and sneakers. His hands were tied behind his back. The man got down from the bus and took a few unsteady steps on the ground. More men followed; they were also blindfolded. A soldier marched them to a field alongside the farm.

The commander assembled his unit and told them that buses carrying civilians from Srebrenica would be brought in. He meant captured Muslim men who had surrendered to the units of Republika Srpska. They are to be executed by our unit, the commander told them. Dražen and his comrades in arms suddenly learned that their squad was to become a firing squad, and he didn't like it at all. Never before had they been assigned such a task. But nobody said a word. Only one of them, Pero, seemed eager to begin, but Dražen noticed that he was drinking from a bottle of brandy. Dražen looked at the prisoners. They were standing with their backs to the soldiers. One man half turned his head toward them, as if he expected something. Was there something he wanted from them? Dražen felt a strong revulsion and was afraid that he would vomit.

No, he would not do it! He couldn't kill men just like that, cold-bloodedly. As he went up to his commander, his hands were trembling. I don't want to do this, he said. Brano Gojković turned his head to Dražen, as if he had not heard him properly. What? he said. Dražen knew the trick. Gojković wanted him to repeat his words loud enough for everybody to hear, so that he would have witnesses for whatever might happen next. Dražen looked at the soldiers. Comrades, I don't want to do this. Are you normal? Do you know what you are doing? he said, but less firmly, feeling his bravery quickly melting away as the others studiously avoided his eyes. Pero openly laughed at him. A moment of awkward silence followed. It occurred to Dražen that he had not heard a single bird singing that day. Gojković looked at Dražen unflinchingly. His expression was serious. Erdemović, he said, if you don't want to do it, walk over there and stand together with the prisoners so that we can shoot you too. Give me your machine gun!

Dražen must have understood instantly that the officer meant what he was saying. But he was confused; he had not expected such a reaction. He had hoped, briefly, that he could get out of this mess if he just said no. What did he expect? He remembered hearing about an earlier case of disobedience, when one soldier was executed by the order of Lieutenant Colonel Milorad Pelemiš, and he realized that now it was too late to say no. He should have said it long ago. His heart was beating so strongly that he could hear nothing but its throbbing. For perhaps a minute or even less, Dražen just stood there with the Kalashnikov machine gun in his hands. For a moment he thought of running into the woods. But he saw the face of his wife before him and felt helpless. They could take revenge on her and the baby at any time. He was responsible for three lives. It was an excuse, yes; the truth was that he had proved to be a coward and he knew it, but what else could he have done? Gojković would not hesitate to order him killed, and Pero would do it with pleasure, although Dražen did not understand what he had against him. Maybe that Dražen was not a pure Serb, which made it even more advisable to take Gojković's threat seriously.

The commander was no longer looking at him, as if he had no further interest in his decision. He ordered the soldiers to take up a position behind the prisoners and the prisoners to kneel on the ground. Dražen took his place at the end of the squad. His heart was still beating loudly when he aimed at an elderly man whose face he luckily enough had not seen before. He quickly, feverishly weighed his options. Of course, he could fire between two prisoners. But his prisoner would still have to be killed. Like having to die twice. Besides, the firing squad was a small one, only a dozen soldiers, and if he didn't aim properly it would be detected immediately. The commander would know, and he would be executed. No, he must aim properly. Then a command came—"Shoot!"—and the man disappeared from his view. He remembered only that his first victim had on a gray T-shirt. Dražen closed his eyes and tried to calm himself. But new prisoners were already in front of him. One of them shouted: "Fuck you, bloody . . ." and did not even have time to finish his sentence before the command to shoot came again. Once he started, Dražen kept shooting every few minutes without thinking much about what he was doing. The only thing he was aware of was trying to aim at elderly people rather than young ones; it seemed less of a waste. Soon the bus was empty.

When Dražen looked at his watch, he was shocked: it had taken them only fifteen minutes to execute some sixty people! A second bus had already arrived. The men in the bus could not see what was awaiting them, as they were blindfolded, too. Dražen was glad for that; he thought this was actually merciful toward these poor men. But pretty soon after that, buses arrived carrying men who were not blindfolded, whose hands were not even tied. It was as though they had been hurriedly pushed into buses and sent to the Branjevo farm. But why such hurry? Dražen did not understand. And there was something more that he did not understand, that did not seem logical to him: the men who came later could surely see what was about to happen to them. They could see dead bodies on the ground and soldiers with Kalashnikovs standing there waiting. And yet they stepped down from the bus and marched to the execution site with two soldiers. Why didn't any of them try to escape into the nearby wood? Dražen wondered. In a couple of minutes one could dive into the safety of those trees; there was at least a slim chance of survival. But not a single prisoner tried to break away. Dražen had never seen such a spectacle before: prisoners walking in orderly fashion to their execution site, like animals in a slaughterhouse. Did they believe somebody would save them? If all of them had tried to run, surely some would reach safety. At the very least, they would die knowing that they had tried. They had nothing to lose. They were to be executed, they must have known it the moment they got off the bus. Dražen wished they would try to run; at least it would give him a reason to shoot at them, and it would be fairer, because they would have had a chance to escape. But no. The prisoners were pouring in in a steady, peaceful stream as if some kind of paralysis had come over them.

Maybe these men no longer felt anything? But then he saw something and realized that this couldn't be. As he aimed at the nape of a man's neck, Dražen saw a treacherous stain on the back of his trousers. There was a wet spot there, getting bigger and bigger. He heard a command and shot once more. When the man fell down, Dražen saw that he was still alive, still urinating out of fear. Dražen was suddenly embarrassed, as if it were happening to him. It could happen to me, too, he thought, but pushed the unpleasant notion away. He was tired and angry with himself, with Gojković, with everybody. It was just not right to execute all these men. If they were soldiers, they were prisoners of war; if they were civilians, what was happening to them was even more unjustified. He and his fellow soldiers were doing something wrong, that much he knew. If there was any justice, these men would not be executed just like that, without a trial, without proof of their guilt. Hundreds of men could not disappear just like that. Their relatives would look for them, and eventually Dražen's unit would be held accountable for their deaths. If Gojković didn't want witnesses, what about his own soldiers? Were they not witnesses to the crime? How could he be sure that nobody would talk?

Just then, Dražen heard a noise. Among the prisoners standing in the field was a man of perhaps sixty, gray-haired and neatly dressed. Don't kill me, he shouted, I saved the lives of many Serbs in Srebrenica. I could give you their names, I am sure they would vouch for me. He started to pull some paper out of his pocket. Dražen approached him and took him aside. He gave him a cigarette and a glass of orange juice. The man sat down and lit the cigarette. His hands were trembling as he handed the paper to Dražen. Here are names and telephone numbers, you can check them if you want, it's true what I am saying . . . But Dražen knew that the man would not be allowed to live, because he was already a witness to the executions. Why did he take him aside, then? Dražen was impressed by this man who had not silently accepted death like the others. He seemed honest and brave, and Dražen wanted to prolong his life for as long as he could. But the man did not look as if he had any hope left. We all used to live together, Muslims, Serbs, Croats, the man said to Dražen. What happened to us, ordinary people? Why did we let it happen? Yes, indeed, what happened to us? Dražen said, If only somebody could explain that to me, if only I knew, but I don't know any more than you do, I am a half-Croat, my wife is a Serb.

Dražen understood that he and the man had something in common: they had nothing against people of other na-

tionalities. But how could you do this? the man asked as he
inhaled the smoke from the cigarette, sensing it would be his
last. What could Dražen tell him but that he did not have a
choice? It sounded like a stupid thing to say to a man about
to lose his life, it sounded damned stupid. But it was the
truth. Dražen was aware that the man was guilty only of being of the wrong nationality; in this, he didn't have a choice,
either.

There was no more time for a conversation. Pero and another soldier approached them and took the man away.
Dražen said no, don't do it, knowing that it was all he could
do. Shut up, don't be stupid, Ivan said. In a minute it was
over; the man was dead.

It must have been past noon, but the soldiers did not have
much time for a break. At the beginning, every half hour
Dražen would go sit under the tree and smoke a cigarette. It
was a kind of escape. But then he no longer craved a smoke.
His movements became more and more mechanical. He
would aim at somebody's head and shoot, and before he had
time to wipe his forehead, the next one would be kneeling in
front of him. He preferred it this way; if he paused too long,
he would become aware of the foul odor of the bodies. In the
heat, bodies started to decompose almost immediately. The
stench reminded him of a butcher's shop. Sometimes his
mother would send him to buy meat, though he tried to
avoid it. In summer the stench in the butcher's shop was unbearable, and fat green flies would land on pieces of raw meat
to eat and lay their eggs. The butcher would entertain himself by catching flies and dropping them in a glass of water.

Dražen would run home, eager to get away from the smell. What a fine nose you have, his mother would tease him. Now the same kind of stench was coming from the field, the same kind of green flies were descending on the fresh bodies.

Ivan, perhaps noticing that Dražen was getting peaked, offered him a brandy, a strong homemade *šljivovica*. Dražen took several sips and felt better. With the alcohol taking over, he could keep shooting for some time without giving himself a chance to think. As he took another long sip of the *šljivovica*, Dražen saw from the corner of his eye a young boy coming down from a bus. The boy was not blindfolded, and Dražen saw his face, though he had promised himself that he would not look at the prisoners' faces, as it made shooting more difficult. The boy might have been fifteen, perhaps younger. His chest was bare, his pale skin exposed to the sun. The boy looked at the soldiers and at the rows of dead bodies in the field. His eyes got bigger and bigger, as if he could not take in all that he saw. But he is a boy, only a boy, Dražen murmured more or less to himself, careful not to stand behind him. When the prisoners kneeled down in front of the squad, just before the command to shoot came, Dražen heard the boy's voice. Mother, he whispered, mother! That day Dražen heard men begging for their lives, grown men crying like children; he heard them promising money, cars, even houses, to the soldiers. Many were cursing, some were sobbing. But this boy was just calling for his mother, as children sometimes do when they awake from a bad dream and all they long for is their mother's hand on their forehead. A minute later the boy was dead, but Dražen was sure that he still could hear his voice. I am beginning to hallucinate, he thought. For the second time that day he felt so nauseated that he had to run to the bushes and vomit. Nothing came out except a yellowish liquid smelling of alcohol.

The next bus had not yet arrived. Dražen leaned against a tree, exhausted. It was already two o'clock. From ten in the morning he had been shooting, trying not to look at the prisoners, trying not to think about them, trying not to feel anything. Now he felt numb, his body as stiff as wood. He felt like a puppet on a string, able only to raise his hands and shoot his gun again and again. He sat there staring at the horizon. He could hear somebody wailing, then a solitary shot. Dražen did not turn his head, he did not want to see anything more, he had had enough of killing. How many more buses would come? After three in the afternoon it was over. Gojković announced that there would be no more arrivals, and they quickly boarded their own bus.

The sun was still high in the sky, and the stench in the air was unbearable. Dražen just had to get away from this nightmarish place. Again, he wanted to jump into water or at least take a shower and wash off the smell of death. If only he could wash his hands! Dražen carefully examined them. There was no blood on them, only a blister on his right index finger. A round, pink blister. How strange, Dražen thought, to get a blister from killing people. He figured he must have fired some seventy times. He had killed perhaps seventy people and got a blister! Suddenly, it was so funny that Dražen laughed hysterically.

Finally they were leaving the Branjevo farm. The field was covered with corpses. Who would bury them? And where? Dražen turned his head away. This was no longer any of his business. He had done his part; for him it was over. For the first time that day he could breathe deeply.

But it was not over. Not yet.

When they arrived in neighboring Pilice, the commander informed them that there were five hundred men in the House of Culture and that they also were to be executed. This time it was easier to say no, because Dražen was not the only one who did. They were all tired from the killing, and they refused to go on. But there were fresh soldiers who volunteered for the task, and the commander accepted them. Dražen sat in a café across from the House of Culture and ordered a strong black coffee. Just before their group arrived, some Muslim men, prisoners in the house, had broken out and been killed as they ran down the street. Some soldiers were still searching the corpses for money and gold. Dražen stared at them, just stared, sipping his coffee. It was too sweet.

Dražen knew that he would never forget this day and that it would remain his curse: the green of the mountain, the blue of the sky, the sound of the first bus coming, the thin man with a mustache, another man's trousers soaked with urine, the stench of rotten meat, the dark red color of blood gushing from a wound, the man who asked him how he could do what he was doing, the boy calling for his mother. He sensed that this day would change his whole life, that it was already changing. He felt tears coming. Boys don't cry, his father used to tell him when he came home with bleeding cuts on his knees. But where was his father now? Where were they all now—his parents, his wife, his friends? Dražen had never felt so alone, alone with twelve hundred dead bodies that would follow him wherever he went.

CHAPTER 9

A Beast in a Cage

The case of Slobodan Milošević, the former president of Serbia and Yu-
goslavia, is the first international prosecution of a former head of state for
crimes committed while in office. He is charged, among other things, with
committing genocide in the war in Bosnia and with crimes against humanity
in the wars in Croatia and Kosovo. Although he most certainly did not kill
anybody himself, he was responsible for the politics that resulted in more than
two hundred thousand dead. Milošević has chosen to defend himself, to act as
his own lawyer at the tribunal.

ONLY A glass wall divided me from Slobodan Milošević
in the courtroom in The Hague. He sat about six to
seven yards away, between two tall UN policemen, close
enough that I could study the expressions on his face, his
body language, and even the details of his clothing. He was
dressed in a dark blue blazer, a pale blue shirt, and a tie in red,
white, and blue—the colors of the Serbian flag. His hair was
completely gray, almost white. His skin was pale, the color of
dough, and he looked unhealthy, as though he had not been
in the sun for some time.

Looking at him, I realized that I was surprised. I cannot say that I felt triumphant, as I had expected I would feel when I finally saw him in the dock. True, I was relieved to see him there, but nevertheless I felt very confused. This bothered me; it even made me angry. I had the privilege of observing the trial of the Butcher of the Balkans, the symbol of evil in my lifetime, the man who set my country on fire—and yet, it was strange to see him in the courtroom.

It made me feel uncomfortable.

I quickly realized what was disturbing me. I had never dared to picture him in a courtroom. Even when he was proclaimed a war criminal, it was hard to imagine that one day he would actually be facing his judges in The Hague. On October 5, 2000, Milošević's party lost the election. When he was arrested soon after, there was a lot of talk about extradition. However, the new Serbian president vehemently rejected the very idea of it. Then three months later the new government, pressed by the need for money, delivered Milošević, just like that. His price was exactly 1.3 billion dollars. He was flown to The Hague. It had, finally, really happened.

Why couldn't I imagine such a development? Why didn't I think of it at all? Now it seems to me that I did not believe in the rule of law. Or that enforcement of the law would be possible in Serbia, especially in Milošević's case. After all, for the decade that he was the president of Serbia and Yugoslavia, he had behaved as if he himself was the law.

I remember—how could I ever forget it?—hearing the news on the radio in my kitchen in Vienna on the morning of April 1, 2001. I was preparing my first espresso coffee of the day with the radio playing in the background, as usual. The news came on; there was something about Milošević. I turned the sound up so as to hear it better. I was expecting news about him; he had been surrounded by the police in his Dedinje residence, and some sort of resolution was expected at any moment. In violent postwar Serbia (and considering his own family history), anything looked possible: he might shoot at the police, the police might shoot at him, he might commit suicide. "Slobodan Milošević surrendered to the police last night, and he is in Belgrade's central prison now," a male voice said on the radio. Surrendered? I stood in my kitchen, incredulous. Was it really true? How was it possible? That morning, the coffee was forgotten.

Almost three months later, on June 26, I watched Christiane Amanpour on CNN in front of the prison in Scheveningen reporting that Milošević was about to land there. I stared at the TV screen as if I had just seen a ghost. Although this possibility had been discussed widely in the world press, I was still not prepared for it. And now here I was, in the courtroom, facing him, seeing him with my very own eyes, again bewildered, again angry with myself because of it. There was something about seeing this man sitting in the courtroom that was incongruous with my memories, with some hidden part of me. Of course I was glad that he was on trial. I was pleased that he would finally have to face justice. But it wasn't that simple. I realized, looking at him, that I was facing the personality cult I had grown up with. I was facing my life in Communist Yugoslavia when I least expected it.

Suddenly I remembered a moment from my childhood. It was when we were living in a small town on the Adriatic coast. It was May 1954, a holiday. It must have been May 1 or perhaps May 25, Tito's birthday, the Day of Youth. My father and I were decorating our window. The window frame had a special nail for hanging Tito's framed portrait. The photograph we had seemed huge to me, although it was probably only about twelve by sixteen inches, perhaps even smaller, as I myself was very small. The portrait showed Tito in the snow-white uniform of a marshal. In those days there was no color photography, at least not in Yugoslavia, so photos were colored by hand. In his desire to make Tito more handsome, the photographer with his brush had gotten carried away. Tito's eyes were too blue, his cheeks too rosy, his mouth too red. When the picture was hung I handed my father several branches of ivy. He laid them loosely under the photo, on two other nails at either end of the window frame. A few red carnations placed here and there, and the decorating was finished. We went into the street to look at it from the outside. Beautiful, isn't it? my father asked me. I nodded. Through the open window we could hear music from our radio. Cheerful marches added to my father's festive mood. I could smell the cake my mother was baking, and I liked our little ceremony even more.

I was just five years old and very proud to be allowed to help my father with such an important task. Our window was the only one in the whole apartment building decorated like this. It was because my father was an army officer, a commander of the local garrison. The picture of Tito surrounded by flowers reminded me of something that I had seen before, but I knew I was not supposed to mention it to my father. It was a secret. My grandma would sometimes take me with her to church. I usually felt a bit sick in the church because of the smell of white lilies, but I was fascinated by it. There I saw pictures and sculptures of Jesus, the Holy Mother, and many saints, and they were all decorated with flowers, too. The decorated picture under our window was very similar to what I had seen in the church, and I thought that Tito, too, must have been a kind of saint in my father's church.

When I was in school, I participated eagerly in celebrating Tito by writing compositions about him, taking part in performances for his birthday, reciting poems about him, and running in relay races in his honor. In our classroom the very same picture of Tito in his snow-white uniform hung above the blackboard, and we garnished it on every state holiday, just as we did at home. As a child, I thought it was normal to celebrate Tito in this way; everyone around me did.

It was years before I learned that in Yugoslavia we were growing up with a personality cult. But what that really meant I saw only when Tito died in 1980. Tito himself did not quite understand that he was dying, as one of the doctors taking care of him in the hospital in Ljubljana later told me. His leg had been amputated and his kidneys did not work, but Tito continued to talk about his plans for the future. Could it be that, once someone has ultimate power, he begins to believe in his own immortality as well? And others begin to believe in it too? After all, Tito had been in power for more than thirty years. It really looked as if he were going to be there forever.

It is easy to think that people in Yugoslavia would be happy to finally get rid of a dictator, which Tito, no doubt, was. But they were not happy. When he eventually died, they were surprised and devastated. I remember men and women crying in the streets for days after his death, wandering around like lost children. His death was a major catastrophe, like an earthquake or a flood. There was a feeling of a terrible loss, of fear of what would happen now, a prevailing atmosphere of despair . . . It was easy for Slobodan Milošević to fill that emotional hunger. People were looking for somebody to take care of them. The orphaned nation needed a new father. When communism collapsed ten years later, people were even more lost, insecure, and frightened, almost like young children forced to start living on their own. Besides, there were no other models of political leadership except for the authoritarian model of Tito.

Slobodan Milošević made his way to the top of the Communist Party structure, mercilessly ousting everybody in his way. But he was not a believer in communism. In 1987 he visited Kosovo Polje, the site of the 1389 battle against the Turks, and delivered his ominous speech to the Kosovo Serbs, who are a minority among the Albanians there. His declaration "No one shall ever beat you again!" quite unexpectedly launched him into the orbit of nationalist heroes. He began to incite Serbian nationalism with his speeches but not because he wanted a war. He was not even a believer; he was not a messianic type of leader like the Croatian president, Franjo Tudjman. His speeches had no fire, no conviction. Most probably, what Milošević believed was that he could control the power of nationalism and manipulate it for his own benefit. He was a skillful demagogue riding on the patriotic feelings of others. The paradox of Milošević is that he was neither a Communist nor a nationalist but an opportunist capable of using any ideology that would help him to remain in power. Opportunism might be his most important characteristic. If it was nationalism that would keep him in power, so be it.

So there he was now, in jail, after thirteen years of being a demigod himself.

I did not expect him to surrender to the police in Belgrade; nobody expected it. I thought there would be some kind of a violent end, like what had happened to Elena and Nicolae Ceausescu in Romania in December 1989: a court-martial followed by a quick execution. I remember well the last speech of Nicolae Ceausescu a few days before his execution. He stood on a balcony of the Communist Party headquarters in Bucharest, addressing a huge mass of people below in the city's main square. Suddenly he heard a strange sound, a sound he was not used to. Instead of applause, for the first time in his life he heard the noise of anger. Comrade Ceausescu did not understand what was going on, one could see it in his face. He was totally surprised. His beloved Romanians! His children! How could they turn on him? I could imagine how Milošević must have felt in those last moments in his house in Belgrade, surrounded by his own police. Surely his people would come to defend him, their beloved leader. But they did not come. People let him down, as they have a habit of doing with dictators.

If Slobodan Milošević and his wife had met a brutal end like the Ceausescus, it would have been fitting: a bloody regime ending in blood. Milošević's victims would have been vindicated, and his followers would have a martyr. Everybody would be pleased. If, on the other hand, he had committed suicide, that would have made sense, too. Much had been written about his parents' suicides, and it was not unrealistic to expect that Milošević would follow suit. But for such a course of action a person has to be brave, have a sense of drama. His suicide could have been a grand departure from the world's stage, a romantic ending, a heroic way to convey to the world that he had no intention of surrendering to his enemies. Milošević could have ensured his place in the memory of the Serbian people and become as beloved as Prince Lazar from the epics about the battle against the Turks at Kosovo Polje. His death might have been a catharsis for the Serbian people, marking the end of authoritarianism.

But Milošević is a bureaucrat. He is simply too small, too ordinary for such dramatic gestures. One explanation why the Serbs turned away from him so quickly following his imprisonment was that they were disappointed in him for just that reason, for allowing himself to be arrested. He was not the person they believed him to be, the hero they had nicknamed Freedom (Slobo-Slobodo). He was just a normal man, afraid for his life. Seeing him surrender like a petty thief must have been humiliating for everybody who believed in him. They had worshiped him as if he were a deity.

And he was just one of them, after all? His surrender made people look childish and foolish, and they were not going to forgive him for that.

Indeed, he really had been beloved in Serbia: three times voted into office in democratic elections, twice as president of Yugoslavia, once as president of Serbia. He ruled like a monarch, as if there were no parliament, prime minister, or democratic procedures of any kind. The only person he sought advice from was his wife, Mira Marković. People in Serbia used to say that their country had two rulers instead of one. As much as they loved him, they hated her, because of her influence on him; but she was protected by him. They were close to each other, to the exclusion of everybody else, almost as though they were an autistic couple whose love for each other carried them further and further from reality.

Now Slobodan Milošević was trying to make up for his failure—that is, for his miserable surrender—with his behavior in the courtroom.

At first, he made quite an impression: he faced the judges alone, without lawyers. He took care to look directly into the cameras, showing no fear or intimidation. He spoke fluently, although not in perfect English, which was his great advantage. Composed and focused, he projected the image of a brave individual caught in an unjust battle. His very first sentence in the tribunal was "I don't recognize this court; this court is a false court, and the indictments are false indictments." He even won some sympathy from the public when Judge Richard May cut him short in the middle of his speech. After all, political speeches were his only interest.

But the judge snapped at him, "Mr. Milošević, will you be quiet, please!" as if scolding a child. Later, Milošević seemed to have lost his nerve. He would shout abuse at the judges, like an angry adolescent.

He denied any wrongdoing on his part. Regarding the war in Bosnia, for example, and alluding to the Dayton Agreement of 1995, he claimed that he had brought peace to Bosnia, not war. We had already seen how far his denial of reality went when he delivered a short speech on TV after signing the capitulation following the NATO bombardment in 1999: Milošević congratulated the Serbs on winning the war. It was like George Orwell's novel *1984*: in Milošević's Serbia lies became truth, war became peace, and defeat became victory.

From his very first appearance at the tribunal, there was a kind of game going on in the courtroom between Milošević and the judges. Milošević would sit with his head turned away from the judges; he avoided looking at them, as if the whole thing had nothing to do with him. He appeared relaxed, uninterested in the long exchanges between the judges and the prosecution about the technical details of the proceedings. Instead, his eyes were screening the public, perhaps looking for familiar faces. At one point, something like a smile appeared on his face, which otherwise showed nothing but contempt. But his relaxed pose was just that: a pose. Like a hunted animal, he was awaiting the ambush. The moment he was given the word, he began to talk with great energy.

"Acting" is the word I would use to describe his behavior in the court. And for a bureaucrat, Milošević is a good actor. The atmosphere in the courtroom instantly changed every time he started to speak; it was evident that he was determined to set the tone of the performance. Perhaps his most significant decision was not to hire a defense lawyer but to represent himself. But he did not defend himself; he delivered political speeches. His wife, Mira Marković, said in an interview, "As my husband does not consider himself guilty, he will not defend himself. He will only speak." Apparently this was a logical decision: you don't need a lawyer to deliver a political speech. A lawyer would not raise political issues. Milošević, on the other hand, was interested only in politics, not in law, not even in the legality or the illegality of the tribunal per se, but in promoting his political goals. He spoke in court because it allowed him to air his own ideas. He could have chosen to defend himself through silence. However, his plan was not to save himself or to reduce his punishment.

Milošević's strategy was transparent from the very beginning: he was in court not to be tried himself, but to put others on trial. There was nothing spontaneous about his performance. It was planned, with two main objectives. First, he would make his trial look like a mock trial. At one of the pretrial hearings he told the judges that they might as well deliver their sentence in advance. Second, he would establish his own "truth," which was that both he and his country were the victims of a conspiracy. Above all, he wanted to be remembered as a champion in defense of his country.

Once he got to say his piece for CNN and the other media, he would throw the truth into their faces. He told the whole world what he thought of the court. He explained that his was, of course, a political trial and that the court was an ille-

gal and a political, not a judicial, institution. He explained
that this was a plot by the most powerful countries to conquer a small, independent Balkan country. He told the world
how hypocritical those Western leaders were, who only yesterday were making deals with him. Back then he wasn't a
war criminal but a "factor of stability." When he refused to
obey their demands, when he did not want to bend to their
wishes and become their slave, his country was bombed and
he was proclaimed a war criminal.

And so he did speak, time after time, on every possible occasion: as he saw it, he was fighting for freedom and independence and against international terrorism. He saw himself as
a kind of Nelson Mandela, one could say, or like Josip Broz
Tito himself. When Tito was put on trial in what was then
the Kingdom of Yugoslavia for his illegal Communist activities, he said, "I recognize only the judgment of my own party."
By copying Tito's attitude—you have got me, all right, I am
your prisoner, but it doesn't mean that I will respect you or
that I will obey your rules—Milošević was behaving like the
leader of the forbidden Communist party in the thirties.

In The Hague, Milošević tried to do what Serbs have always been good at: presenting themselves as victims of historical events, plots, misunderstandings, and the wrongdoings
of others. And these court appearances gave him the chance
to demonstrate his extraordinary ability to adapt to any new
situation and use it to his advantage. The courtroom was an
international stage, he realized, and because of the media, he
could play his role before the world. He knew a bit about the
importance of the media. When he took power in 1987, he

immediately got rid of all the chief editors of the important newspapers and the heads of the television and radio stations. From then on the media was strictly controlled—and was his main instrument for maintaining power over a decade.

Milošević needs a public. He needs it at home, though he is probably not fully aware of how little support he now has. He probably still believes that he is addressing huge masses of his followers, although the majority of Serbs have already forgotten him. Also, as a dedicated politician, Milošević has borrowed James Bond's credo: "Never say never." In the volatile political situation in Serbia and in the world in general, he thinks he may yet have a chance to seize power again. The fact that he is in jail doesn't interfere with his intentions. That situation can change as quickly as it does in the James Bond movies.

He needs the public abroad even more. As long as he is at the center of attention, he has the opportunity to put forward his version of history. This is his most important task at the trial in The Hague. He has to convince people that black is white, and this he will have a chance to do only if he has access to the media. His main endeavor now, as it has long been, is not to present events as they really happened but to create history, just as he earlier created reality.

• • •

The more I watched him in the courtroom, day after day, and the more intimate I became with his gestures—his eyes scanning the public, his grimaces, his movements, his tics—the more I realized that I didn't know anything about this

man. After all, he was not only one of the biggest villains of
the twentieth century, but he also changed my life. I cannot
but wonder who Slobodan Milošević really is. What kind of
person is hiding behind that aggressive attitude, that pale
face, that stream of words? Who is the man behind the actor,
behind the politician? Interestingly, I did not feel the need to
know what was behind Tito's public face; what we saw was
good enough for me. Milošević is a very private person, but
that fits well the authoritarian model: both Tito and Stalin
were secretive about their private lives as well.

So much has been written about Milošević, but mostly
about his political career and his role in the war. It is known
that his parents ended their lives themselves, that he met his
wife very early, that he has two children and few friends, and
that he cares very deeply only about his family. Not much
beyond that is known, certainly not enough for us to understand what makes him tick. It is almost as if this man has no
personality other than his public one.

I read four biographies of Slobodan Milošević and the diary of his wife, Mira Marković, in the hope of understanding
the motives of the man. But every new biography added to
my disappointment. The books by Dusko Doder, Florance
Hartmann, Slavoljub Djukić, and Vidosav Stefanović focus
on just one or two aspects of him: his climb to the presidency
and his role in the war. They are political biographies. Still,
from time to time there emerges a shrewd, merciless, unsen-
timental Communist Party bureaucrat who is, above all, an
opportunist.

What I missed in these biographies of Milošević was the other side of him, his private face. It seemed his biographers could touch only his surface, the shell, not the essence of the man. The four books provide no details about his behavior behind the public scene, about his relations with other people, his collaborators, his friends, his wife or children—anything that would give us an idea about who he really is.

We, the public, are convinced that persons like him—important persons, political leaders, even when they are villains—must be interesting in their private lives as well. We want to know why they act as they do, and we believe we might find their motives and reasons for their decisions in their biographies. But when one experienced journalist after another seems unable to reach any other dimension of Milošević, it makes me wonder: what if there is nothing to write about?

What is most revealing of Milošević's personality are perhaps his own words. In the spring of 2002 the Croatian weekly *Globus* published a series of transcripts of his conversations taped by the Croatian secret police between 1995 and 1998. The conversations took place in the Karadjordjevo hunting lodge, a luxurious residence just outside Belgrade where Tito used to wine and dine his foreign guests, and they include exchanges with the president of Serbia, Milan Milutinović; Milošević's brother, Bora (the Serbian ambassador in Russia); and other members of his family. There are two striking things about the conversations. First, Milošević, by then the president of Yugoslavia, gives direct orders to Milutinović and calls the chief editor of *Politika* (the leading Serbian daily) to tell him what to write about and how to write it. The other astonishing thing is the vulgarity of his language. Milošević's every second word is "fuck," as if he were incapable of expressing himself in any other way.

Conversations with his wife and his children take up the greatest part of the transcripts. Though the family is close, Marija and Marko grew up as typical kids of powerful parents. Marko became famous for his connections to gangsters and for murky business deals that made him rich; Marija for her liking of guns and gangsters and her habit of picking her lovers from her bodyguards.

Milošević calls his wife "baby," and she calls him "beauty." He tells his son when he wants to have plastic surgery that he is "as beautiful as his father," and he expresses irritation at his daughter's latest boyfriend. But more telling, it seems to me, the transcripts actually give the same picture of Slobodan Milošević as his four biographers do. There is nothing interesting about him as a private person, period. The transcripts, like the biographies, reveal what there is to reveal about this man: banality, vulgarity, and emptiness. There is no elegance or grandeur about him, not a single interesting thought, nothing to inspire curiosity. All in all, Milošević appears to be just a boring character surrounded by corrupt children and a wife thirsty for power. In history, he may have played a gigantic role, the role of a villain, but he appears to be a dwarf. A small, angry, autistic man. Deserted by his followers, now behind bars.

What illustrates his character best, perhaps, is an episode

from the court. At the end of his cross-examination of a prosecution witness, Nikola Samardžić, Milošević asked him if he was familiar with the Serbian proverb "People who lie have short legs." The public and judges were astonished. An awkward moment of silence fell on the courtroom, as if no one could believe what Milošević had just said. Everybody present, including Milošević, of course, knew that the witness Samardžić indeed had short legs. Not because he was a liar but because he had had them amputated due to complications from diabetes. Day after day he entered the courtroom slowly, cautiously, with the help of a cane. But this meant nothing to Milošević. He could not restrain himself from making a cruel joke. This was not because he had poor taste. The reason was much deeper. To Milošević, another man's suffering means nothing. He can feel no empathy for the others. And he made me understand for the first time a definition of evil that I read somewhere long ago: *evil is the absence of empathy.*

When I saw him for the last time in the courtroom, it was evident that he was becoming increasingly agitated. He was furious. He moved back and forth in his seat. He took his jacket off. He pulled faces. He tried to speak but was silenced by the judge. He stopped speaking English and would speak only Serbian; perhaps he had grown too frustrated to keep taking the time to show off. At the beginning he had made me feel like a child visiting the zoo. I was watching a once-dangerous wild animal now in captivity, and I felt thrilled but also a little uneasy, awestruck but apprehensive, incredulous at being so close to the beast, almost close enough to touch it. Maybe Milošević did not realize it yet, but this was exactly what his situation had come to: that of a beast in a cage. This man who himself had not lifted a finger in violence but whose decade-long murderous nationalist politics threw Yugoslavia into a whirlpool of death and chaos is responsible for the deaths of more than two hundred thousand people.

CHAPTER 10

Ribbons and Bows

Mirjana Mira Marković is the wife of the longtime president of Serbia and Yugoslavia, Slobodan Milošević. A professor of sociology at the University of Belgrade, for more than a decade she was the most influential person in Milošević's life, directly influencing his political decisions and determining the destiny of many. Because of this, she was the most feared woman in Serbia and earned the nickname Lady Macbeth. Although she considered herself an academic, a writer, and an intellectual, she had political ambitions and was the president of the JUL (Yugoslav United Left) Party. In February 2003 she fled to Russia; she was sought by the Serbian police because of her suspected involvement in the death of Milošević's opponent Ivan Stambolić, whose body was found on March 28.

EVERY TIME I see a photo of Mira Marković, Slobodan Mi-lošević's wife, or her image on a TV screen, I feel the urge to tell her that her hair and her dresses are so hopelessly unfashionable that she must do something about them. Not that I am myself a fashion slave. But she looks so far from stylish or even tasteful. Perhaps she is not aware of how old-fashioned she looks, or perhaps she doesn't care. But I can't help wondering why she chooses to dye her hair so black and wear it in a style that looks more like a helmet or a wig than a hairdo? The severe color only hardens her face and makes her wrinkles look deeper. She can read in any women's magazine that strong, dark colors make you look older and that the older a woman becomes, the lighter she should color her hair. But perhaps as an intellectual and a feminist, Mira Marković doesn't read such superficial magazines? That's too bad; it might put her in tune with her time.

After all, I can only assume that she would like to look younger, just as the rest of us would. If this were not the case, she would certainly wear her hairdo in some other style, not with bangs or fringes. Bangs are for girls and young women. We wore them in the late fifties and early sixties. At that time, there was but one film magazine, *Filmski svijet* (*The World of Film*), which was our window to the world of fashion and glamour. We collected pictures of film stars, exchanged them, and glued them into albums. Many film stars of that time had bangs, like Brigitte Bardot and Audrey Hepburn. But the most striking bangs were worn by Elizabeth Taylor in her role as Cleopatra. Perhaps Mira saw the hairstyle years ago in the cinema in Požarevac, or perhaps she, too, read *Filmski svijet,* and the bangs impressed her so strongly that she has never been able to stop wearing them. Nowadays, because of her hair she still looks like Cleopatra, except that she is not Elizabeth Taylor. And Elizabeth Taylor herself doesn't wear bangs anymore.

Where else could young Mira get the ideas on how to do her hair or how to dress? In the fifties and sixties only a few people in my country had a television set at home. The programs were in black and white—we couldn't get color TV for many years after it was invented—and in Yugoslavia one could see only foreign shows. Our neighbors had a television set; when they watched it, usually on Saturdays, the whole neighborhood would congregate in their living room to watch. Italian entertainment programs were very spectacular, with elegant hosts and hostesses and dancing girls dressed in beautiful, glittering dresses. We girls—and our mothers— were flabbergasted by all that glitz, and we got all kinds of ideas about fashion and beauty right from the TV screen. If we saw a dress we wanted, we would have to describe it to a seamstress or sew it ourselves. My mother was very good at that, at turning coats inside out or making children's clothes from old grown-up clothes. And she was also capable of making a fine evening dress out of an ordinary piece of cloth. Although there were no fashion boutiques at the time, thanks to her skill and imagination she was always well dressed.

There was, of course, a place women could shop, called NAMA, or People's Store, the very first chain of department stores in Yugoslavia. I remember the one in Rijeka. My mother did not buy her clothes there, but I loved visiting it because it was the biggest store in town and there were all kinds of interesting things to see there. What fascinated me most of all were the mannequins of women and men and even children in the shop window. I suppose they were made of plaster, with painted eyes and mouths and painted hair as well, kind of weird sculptures. There they stood, stiff and motionless, dressed in clothes that hung sadly on them fixed with pins behind their backs.

When I look at Mira Marković, I can't help think of standing in front of the old NAMA shop window. Except for the fact that she is not thin but plump, she looks like a mannequin that just stepped out of the window display wearing a shapeless little two-piece set in dark blue or a huge blouse with a small print in a lighter color, made of cheap material and badly cut. As if the function of her clothes were just to hide her body. My spinster aunt would wear baggy clothes, too (it's funny to think that she was considered a spinster at the age of thirty-eight, but that is another story). My aunt also wore orthopedic shoes. My mother probably should have had orthopedic shoes herself because she had flat feet, but she would never have dreamed of wearing them. She liked shoes with extremely high heels, like elegant sandals made of black patent leather. Good shoes were difficult to come by in the old Yugoslavia. Once or twice a year my mother would go to Trieste to buy them, and I would accompany her. Then she had to smuggle them back into the country. She never had any trouble, though: she would simply put them on. It always worked.

I doubt that Mira ever went to Trieste; it is too far from Požarevac. She was probably sentenced to wear terrible Borovo shoes—the kind of shoes worn by waitresses, hairdressers, and other women whose jobs require them to be on their feet all day—until she became the first lady. By then, perhaps, she had gotten used to them.

Her whole style demonstrates that she grew up in a Communist country and is still used to the fashion that was created for postwar *drugarice;* that is, female comrades during

Communist times. This style was characterized by its distinct lack of femininity, as if women were advised to look more like men or at least neutral. The message was that they could hold responsible jobs and positions only at the expense of their femininity, so women consciously played it down—that is, if they had any (and sometimes one really had reasons to doubt it!). Maybe Mira Marković subconsciously adopted that "comrade" style. Or perhaps she thought that if women were equal to men, they did not need to make an effort to look nice.

But I strongly doubt that this is the case with her. There is one thing about her that indicates that she is not only extremely feminine but also quite coquettish. Mira Marković seems to like to wear some sort of decoration in her hair—a plastic flower, a ribbon, a bow—often in a bright color, in contrast to her drab clothes. Such accessories have become her personal trademark. Her bows remind me of my childhood. All women of my generation were photographed as babies wearing bows. When I was small there was the custom—which probably died out with my generation—of making an "official" photo of a baby. The baby was usually about a year old when it was taken to the photographer (very few people had cameras). It would be undressed and put on its belly on a piece of cloth or a fur. The child would prop itself up with its hands and lift its head up, often displeased with such an uncomfortable position. If it was a girl, the mother would tie a bow onto the baby's thin hair. Bows and ribbons were still fashionable in the late fifties, when Mira probably began wearing them. I was no exception: before I went to school in the morning, my grandmother would comb my long hair in two plaits and decorate it with two big white bows like butterflies. Later I wore ribbons in my hair, too, but that was in the sixties, and the ribbons were just to hold my hair back.

Why would Mira Marković wear flowers, ribbons, and bows as a teenager would? There is a story behind the plastic flower that she used to wear in the nineties. Mira was brought up by her maternal grandparents. Her mother was killed when Mira was only eight months old. All her life she was stigmatized because of her mother's terrible faith: it was said that her mother had denounced her Belgrade Communist Party colleagues while being tortured in prison by the Germans. Her father, a high party functionary and a war hero, did not acknowledge Mira until she was fifteen years old. They were never close, nor did she ever become friendly with her three half sisters and her half brother. Her mother's destiny greatly influenced young Mirjana; she took her mother's name, Mira, as her nickname. Not only could she not accept that her mother had committed treason; she also took revenge on anyone who believed that it was true, even her own father. Mira idealized her mother as a pure and committed Communist. Once she came across a photo of her wearing a flower in her hair. After that, in memory of her, Mira would often wear a plastic flower in her hair, too.

But why a bow? Today the bow in Mira's hair looks totally incongruous with her matronly appearance. In fact, it looks grotesque. Can it really be only a matter of bad taste? Why would she want to look like this?

The moment she starts to speak, everything falls into place. In a way, her voice explains her looks. One expects a deep, strong, almost masculine voice that would be in accordance with her coarse features or at least the voice of a woman of a certain age. But her voice comes as a complete surprise; for a moment, one wonders if it is genuine. She has a high-pitched, childish voice, the voice of a teenage girl. Besides this, she lisps like a child who never learned how to speak properly. And the more nervous she gets, the more evident is her lisping.

As I look at her and listen to her voice—in an interview she is giving on television—I think of the wooden Russian babushka dolls, one inside the other. To me, Mira is like that, one person inside another. This extraordinary voice does not belong to the heavily built middle-aged woman that we see on the outside but to the little girl inside. That girl, in fact, is the real Mira as she sees herself and, more important, as her husband sees her: not a sixty-year-old woman but a sixteen-year-old girl with bangs and ribbons. She wants to look and sound as she did when she and Slobodan Milošević met and fell in love at the high school in Požarevac in 1958. Under Mira's magic spell, time has stood still for both of them.

The fragile girl inside Mira needs protection. When she, with her young voice, turns to Slobodan, he is unable to resist. And if he tries to resist, she bursts into tears. Like a little girl, she plays games with him, crying not because she feels grief but to get her way. This is part of her spoiled-girl repertoire, or at least this is what people who know them say about her. Slobodan still seems to see her as she was in high school: a young, insecure, not very pretty, lonely, and helpless little girl. Helpless, that is, until she met him.

Slobodan could understand her because he too was from a broken family. His father left him, his older brother, and his mother, who was a teacher, and went to Montenegro. Slobodan grew up a lonely, serious boy without friends. He was a good pupil, one of those who sits in the front row of the classroom and listens attentively but does not participate in sports or other such activities. Slobodan and Mira met in December 1958, when she was sixteen and he was seventeen. From that time, Mira was no longer "afraid of the dark, the cold, or of getting poor marks for mathematics," as she wrote in one of her books.

Since then they have been inseparable. They became so devoted to each other, so absorbed with each other, that people in Požarevac used to call them Romeo and Juliet. To me, however, they are more like Hansel and Gretel, two little children deserted by their parents. As in the fairy tale, they have managed to save themselves. But they still live in the wild and threatening woods and perceive themselves as two abandoned orphans clinging to each other in order to survive. Tragedy in Slobodan's family brought them even closer together. When he was a student in his early twenties, his father committed suicide. Ten years later, his mother hanged herself. But Slobodan and Mira still had each other. They did not need other people. The world could no longer touch them.

Today he probably sees in her the same vulnerability and

helplessness and still rushes to protect her. But when I look at her, I see a shrewd, calculating, cold woman, not vulnerable at all and certainly not helpless. But this is beside the point, because neither of them cares a hoot about how other people see them. They care only about each other. In fact, they go through life as if there are no other people. When we are young we often imagine that ideal love is when you find a soul mate, someone who almost becomes part of you. Someone you can trust absolutely, who will never let you down. Most of us soon realize that love isn't like this. Occasionally we see couples who seem to have such a relationship, but there is usually something odd about them, as though they are encased in their own little cocoon, afraid to leave it. The longer they have been together, the more alienated from the world they seem to be.

Mira and Slobodan are completely devoted to each other and to their children, and nobody outside their little autistic haven can touch or move them. Only she could turn this cold, calculating man into a caring and tender person. After about forty years together, they still call each other names like "pussycat" and hold hands when they go for a walk. People close to them—there are not many, and they don't like to talk—swear that he has never been unfaithful to her. Once, allegedly, a secretary made a pass at Slobodan. He shouted at her, "This is not a brothel!"

In his office Milošević displayed only one photo, that of Mira, his wife. Indeed, it is not possible to write about him without taking into consideration his wife's influence, as it is not possible to write about her and her achievements without mentioning that she is married to Slobodan Milošević. They function only as a couple, as two parts of a whole. They derive power from each other, creating a relationship that excludes everybody else, and their behavior eventually brought Milošević to where he is now—on trial in The Hague. He, a party apparatchik, was willing to pay any price to remain in power. She supported him unconditionally. When her Slobodan discovered nationalism as a means of remaining in power, she stood by him. When he became a populist dictator, she still stood by him. Her support was all that he needed.

Mira is the key to Slobodan: she is the one that makes him tick. She is the driving force behind him, the ambitious other half that pushed this colorless party bureaucrat to grasp every opportunity for power. As is sometimes the case with couples who have been married for a long time, they also have begun to look more and more alike. Small dark eyes, thin lips, broad coarse faces, and two deep lines from their noses to the corners of their mouths pulling their faces down with gravity. But they are still different in many ways. In photographs he never smiles; she often does. She is communicative, he is reclusive; she is vain, he is not; she is ambitious, he is an opportunist; she cares about her image, he does not; she is an aspiring intellectual, he is a bureaucrat. However, the insatiable hunger for power is something they have in common.

Mira Marković was not satisfied with just being first lady. She wanted more. A reader can conclude that simply by studying the dust jacket of her book *Between East and South,* published in Belgrade in 1996. On it she is described as a tenured professor on the natural science and mathematics faculty of the University of Belgrade, a member of the Russian Academy of Sciences, an honorary professor of Lomonosov University, a director of the International Center for Sociopolitical Research of Slavic Countries at the Russian Academy, and an editor of two Russian-Yugoslav professional periodicals. Mirjana Marković is also the author of three sociology books and has published two volumes of her newspaper columns. Very much like Elena Ceausescu, the wife of the Romanian president, she never hid her ambition of becoming both a prominent public figure and a leading intellectual. One of her cronies, a journalist from the daily newspaper *Politika,* in his desire to please Milošević, has described her as "one of the most important and interesting personalities of the scientific elite in the world." In an autocratic society such as Serbia, honors and titles are not difficult to achieve, especially if you are the wife of the president.

But this was not enough to satisfy Mira's ambition. She wanted to participate in politics directly, not merely through her husband, no matter how great an influence that gave her. In 1994 she founded a left-wing party called the JUL (Yugoslav United Left). This enabled her to operate in the same political arena as her husband. Soon the JUL had considerable influence in Serbian politics. Membership in her party was known to be a shortcut to a good political position. Interestingly, Mira wanted to maintain a modest image, so she refused the position of president of the party, taking only the post of executive manager. But this did not fool anyone.

Mira always maintained a veneer of femininity and rarely

demanded outright that her husband should do this or that; rather, she seduced him to do what she wanted. Milošević is a man madly and blindly in love with his wife, so, eyewitnesses say, it did not take much to persuade him; a look, a gesture, the tone of her voice was enough. Moreover, he truly considers Mira to be a political and scientific genius. He was the most avid reader of her newspaper columns and willingly believed the critics who praised Mira's literary style and clever analysis.

I can hardly imagine that Mira would have risen to the position of an influential arbiter in Serbian society on her own merits as a Marxist professor of sociology. But the one who commands a powerful man is even more powerful than he himself is; as Mira wrote in one of her books: "If a woman is capable of destroying the best man; if she—in spite of her average capacities—is capable of engaging better people than herself to turn her into a successful personality—then she deserves to enter a new century as his ruler." Indeed, Serbia had not one ruler but two. The fact is that Mira was able to make use of her position as the wife of the powerful man through the pathological hold she had on her besotted husband.

Mira Marković sees herself as a feminist. This is why she kept her family name. She often says that women are the stronger sex, but at the same time she likes to present herself as a romantic, delicate, sensitive soul with a special affinity for the arts: an aspiring writer and a lover of music. Full of contradictions, she is a Marxist and, until recently, was a member of the Communist Party, but she also believes in astrology. Her husband is proud of her independence and her intellectual achievements. With his unreserved support, she began to believe she was important not only for him, but for the whole world as well.

In her book *Between East and South,* which is actually a diary she kept from 1994 to 1996, she proclaims her opinions on all kinds of subjects, ranging from garden flowers, wild birds, her children, and the weather to analyses of her political opponents. She often writes in a quasi-poetic style combining moralistic views and truisms: "I always asked myself why birds return from the south when they fly there in the autumn. Is that because of a desire to fly to the north, or because of the hope that, for once, the autumn would not replace the summer there?" Her sentences contain sweeping, empty generalizations, such as the following: "The material and spiritual development is in a constant state of advance, an advance even faster as time goes by." The only really interesting thing about this book is that she hardly mentions the ongoing war in Bosnia. When she says anything about war at all, it is to lament human nature: "Above all the dead and wounded people one question hovers, the question without answer—why? Why are they dying, why are they disappearing, why have they lost their parents, children, friends, why are they wounded, why are they without houses and homeland, why do people behave like animals more than bloodthirsty animals themselves?" If I did not know who the author was, I would think these were the words of a naïve teenager, not someone with credentials to carry out political analysis. But written by Slobodan Milošević's wife, such words are sheer cynicism because she deliberately chooses not to acknowledge her husband's role in what she calls "bloody orgies." This was the time when Sarajevo was still under the siege and snipers were killing people lining up for water or bread. In July 1995 the UN-protected enclave of Srebrenica fell and the soldiers of Republika Srpska troops executed seven thousand Muslim men. In her diary from this time, Mira Marković doesn't mention it.

I imagine her sitting at her desk, looking out at her garden and writing about birds and clouds. After all, she herself did not see the dead or refugees there. Nor, according to her own words, did she speak about them with her husband. Mira Marković was widely read in Serbia but not because of her eloquent style or her brilliant thoughts. Her column, published in a biweekly magazine called *Rainbow,* was read as a kind of political horoscope. It was common knowledge that if she criticized someone in her column, his or her career would soon be over. If Milošević disliked somebody and wanted to eliminate him politically, he would have Mira do the job. This was what happened to Mihajlo Marković. A well-known philosopher (no relation to Mira) and a member of a group of critics of Marxism around the periodical *Praxis,* he was the most prominent member and chief ideologist of Milošević's Socialist Party. But he supported Radovan Karadžić and Republika Srpska at a time when Milošević wanted to cut off all ties to them, so he had to be punished. The same happened to Borisav Jović, the former president of Yugoslavia, and Milorad Vučelić, the head of Serbian television. Milošević stripped them of their party ranks with no explanation in a seventeen-minute conference. The explanation had already been given in one of his wife's columns.

It was not only people in politics who feared Mira. In Karadjordjevo, when Milošević and his wife were celebrating New Year's Eve in 1995, the electricity was cut off for several hours because of a technical problem. Mira wrote in her column that she believed it was an act of revenge arranged by political opponents who ruled Belgrade at the time. As a consequence, the entire managerial board of the electric company was replaced overnight. A more tragic—to put it mildly—episode involved a journalist named Slavko Ćuruvija. He was Mira's friend until he had the audacity to tell her that Serbia, under the flag of the JUL and the Radical Party, was becoming a fascist country. Mira reacted vehemently in her column, calling him a traitor. A few months later he was murdered in broad daylight while walking down the street with his wife. Nobody could prove that Ćuruvija's murder had anything to do with Mira's condemnation of him, though perhaps people reading her columns were inspired to take justice into their own hands. But it seems more likely that it was a secret police operation. Knowing the modus operandi of the Milošević-Marković family, many strongly suspected that there was indeed a connection.

Likewise, anyone who was praised by Mira could expect promotion in the near future. Because of her arbitrary judgments and her profound influence over her husband, she was feared and hated even more than he was. She was Milošević's main, if not his only, political adviser. For a man who liked to decide everything single-handedly, as if state institutions did not exist, he depended heavily on her opinions. His biographers agree that she had such a hold on her husband that some of his political opponents used to whisper that he was under petticoat rule. Therefore, although she was not indicted by the tribunal in The Hague, she bears at least a moral responsibility for his deeds.

Mira Marković was interviewed by Tim Sebastian on BBC TV in September 2001, not long after Milošević was extradited to the tribunal in The Hague. It is an extraordinary display. Dressed in a black skirt and a black blouse with white polka dots that could have come from my aunt's wardrobe, she sits stiffly in her chair, like a caricature of Cleopatra. During the entire half-hour program, she doesn't show a single emotion; the expression on her face never changes, even when her words are angry. The only things that move are her pudgy hands, her nails polished bright red and her fingers adorned with huge rings. From time to time she touches her hair with a coquettish gesture.

Mira never actually answers a single question. Maybe she is not even listening to the questions. She must have agreed to do the interview so that she could tell the world what she thought. She is not about to answer unpleasant questions put by some journalist. Tim Sebastian, for example, wants to know why Slobodan Milošević since his arrest continues to insist that the tribunal is illegal. "Milošević did not object to the tribunal when Radovan Karadžić and Ratko Mladić were indicted," he points out. Mira retaliates viperously: "Would you, please, behave as a journalist and an intellectual! You are interrogating me as if I were in a court! I did not accept the invitation to talk to you in order to feel uncomfortable but, as you said, in order that you could inform your public about an alternative opinion."

As the interview goes excruciatingly on, it becomes increasingly clear that Mira is a person who does not tolerate debate. She is deeply offended by Sebastian's questions, and instead of answering she lectures him about the nineteen countries plotting against Yugoslavia and her heroic husband who "fought for freedom and independence. . . . Our responsibility for that bloodshed is minor. The responsibility should be borne by those outside of Yugoslavia who financed this bloodshed." When Sebastian asks her, very politely, the obvious question—does she believe that her husband will be released from The Hague—she arrogantly brushes it aside. "I don't want to answer that question! And don't look at me like that, I am not in a police station!" Confronted with such rudeness, Tim Sebastian, an experienced journalist who has interviewed all kinds of people, appears completely at a loss.

Mira Marković as professor, party leader, and first lady, is not used to being questioned and certainly not to being contradicted. Her behavior on the BBC echoes Milošević's performance in the courtroom. He will not listen to questions either, and when allowed to speak, he preaches on the illegality of the court and the international powers destroying his small independent country. In the BBC interview, Mira repeats his words—or perhaps Milošević is repeating her words at the tribunal; it is hard to say. They both behave as people who have no doubt that they are in the right. And she reacts in exactly the same way as Milošević at the tribunal: at first cool and composed, she becomes angrier and angrier (and consequently lisps more and more) as Tim Sebastian refuses to accept her diatribes and insists on proper answers. Obviously she is not accustomed to such treatment, and so she is shocked and put out. How dare he question her like that? Or rather, she is accustomed to Communist-style journalism: a politician delivers a message, no questions asked. The press is there to spread that message or, as Mira puts it, "the truth."

Milošević was in shock too. He did not believe that he could be arrested, he did not believe that he could be extradited to the International Tribunal, and he probably did not believe that he would ever actually be questioned. He was above all that. Both Mira Marković and Slobodan Milošević are used to preaching, not listening, to others. To offend them is to tell them to be quiet, to prevent them from talking. At the end of the interview, Mira tries another method on Sebastian, the one she uses on her husband: feminine helplessness. In her most girlish voice she accuses Tim Sebastian of not behaving toward her as a gentleman and a "gallant knight." It is an astonishing moment, because her use of the word "knight" reveals the world she is living in. It is a fairy-tale world, populated by knights and dragons, by witches and fairies, and surely by princesses, too. In her world, knights show respect for ladies and the prince and the princess live happily ever after.

Milošević and Mira's world is far removed from the outside world and impervious to reality. The Serbian journalist

Slavoljub Djukić, in his biography entitled *On, ona i mi* (*Him, Her and Us*), writes that for Milošević and his wife "reality has no importance at all." Because they had power, they created their own reality; this is what power meant to them. They still see themselves not as they really are but as they want each other to be—and want others to see them. She is a brilliant intellectual, a great mind, and his vulnerable little girl. He is a brilliant politician, a man of principles, a freedom fighter, and her strong and capable husband. Now that the whole world is against them, they try even harder to shield each other from reality.

There is an air of tragedy about this couple. They have not met with the same violent end as the Ceausescus, but they suffer from the same affliction. They have no conception of the idea that people have to pay for their deeds in one way or another. They refuse—or are perhaps unable—to understand why all this is happening to them. If reality does not adjust to their ideas, well then, so be it. So much the worse for reality—until reality finally, brutally, intruded into their lives.

Slobodan and Mira are truly like Hansel and Gretel. Unloved, abandoned, but united in their own autistic world. When they wielded enormous power they were dangerous to everyone. Now they can harm only themselves.

CHAPTER II

Punished by the Gods

General Ratko Mladić, a commander of the Republika Srpska forces, and Radovan Karadžić, the former president of the Republika Srpska—the Serbian republic in Bosnia—have been charged by the tribunal for crimes of genocide, crimes against humanity, grave breaches of the Geneva Convention, and violations of the laws and customs of war in Bosnia between 1992 and 1995. As the result of these crimes, approximately two hundred thousand Bosnian Muslims lost their lives. Both men are also charged with occupation of the "safe area" of Srebrenica and ordering summary executions of more than seven thousand Muslim men. Mladić and Karadžić, considered the biggest war criminals after Slobodan Milošević, are still at large and in hiding.

I‌T WAS spring, and General Ratko Mladić was cutting roses in his garden in Belgrade. Cutting, pruning, mowing, watering—gardening had been his only task for years. Nine years after the peace treaty in Bosnia, he was a general without an army, a man without a job. Nobody, except the tribunal in The Hague, was interested in this Butcher of Bosnia. When he was not occupied in his garden, attending a soccer game, or eating at a restaurant, Mladić drank heavily. He frequently visited the graveyard where his daughter, Ana, is buried. At sixty years of age, Mladić was a psychological wreck. He no longer had anything to look forward to. He was a man of the war, and the war was now in the past.

Moreover, the new, post-Milošević Serbian government had deprived him of the bodyguards that used to protect him. In 2002, because of the pressure of the tribunal on the Serbian government to arrest him, he was forced to leave his gardening and go into hiding.

Reality had finally caught up with him.

General Mladić fought on two fronts and lost on both. The first was in Bosnia. After five years of fighting and conquering 70 percent of Bosnian territory, he had to withdraw his troops in accordance with the Dayton Agreement of November 1995. Republika Srpska got 49 percent of the Bosnian territory, but the Serbs from that territory were forced to live in an official federation together with Muslims and Croats.

The second front—of which he was perhaps not even aware—was in his own home. Because the real story about Mladić is not the one of his victories and losses on the battlefield; the real story about him is that of his personal tragedy: his daughter's suicide. That for years he had been a part of Serbian mythology could not help him when it came to his family. When Ana committed suicide in March 1994, his life turned from a classic Serbian myth into a classic Greek tragedy. It is the only time I have ever felt sorry for the general.

The night before his daughter's suicide, Mladić's wife, Bosa, his son, Darko, and Ana were playing Sinking Ships after dinner. This somehow moved me, reminding me of my own childhood, although Ana was a twenty-three-year-old student of medicine and Darko just a couple of years younger. Sinking Ships is a childish game I used to play with my father when I was about eight years old, when there was no television. After dinner my grandmother would bring out a box with all kinds of games, and we would sit and play until late at night. A radio would hum in the background. My father would be listening to the news, or we would all listen to the program for sailors, which had mothers or wives ordering their favorite songs for Marko on his way to Singapore or Peter on his way back from Costa Rica. My younger brother, who was too small to play with us, would sit in our grandma's lap and cheer for me. I loved these moments when the whole family was engaged in the game, forgetting their daily grudges. But this was long ago, when I was a child.

I imagine that nostalgic scene in Mladić's house as well, the four members of his family sitting around their kitchen table. Jokes and Ana smiling, determined to win the game. Yet there is something strange about it, something that bothers me when I try to picture the scene. Something is wrong. Why would a brother and a sister who were no longer children play a childish game with their parents?

• • •

Mladić is a stocky man with a big head and a bull's neck. While he talks in the sharp, imposing voice of someone who is used to issuing commands, his reddish face glistens with sweat. His looks suggest that he enjoys earthly pleasures, such as food and drink. He probably loves sausages, roasted piglet and lamb, *ćevapčići* (spicy meatballs), and *sarma,* the latter two being Turkish specialties, of course, though one probably shouldn't point that out to him. But without what the Turks left behind in Serbia after five hundred years of occupation, there wouldn't be much in the way of a Serbian cuisine. And a lot of food in Serbia is seasoned with hot red pepper, which calls for drinking *rakija,* the strong homemade local brandy made from plums. Every uniform looks too small on Mladić, as if it might burst at any moment. His red face indicates that his blood pressure is too high, and he probably suffers from high cholesterol. In short, he looks not so much like a soldier as a good candidate for a heart attack.

Yet it was not so long ago that his name was a synonym for fear to thousands of Muslims in Bosnia, so powerful was this man. Mladić was the person who kept Sarajevo besieged for three years, a city where he had a house and where his mother and his friends used to live, a city that he knew well. Twelve thousand people were killed in Sarajevo before he had to withdraw his forces. Then he moved on to Goražde and Srebrenica.

In Sarajevo people who know him told me that he is a frightful person. It was General Mladić who made me understand how the fall of the UN-protected enclave of Srebrenica was possible: the fleeing of the Dutch UN corps, the days of massacre that followed, the exodus of thirty thousand women and children.

I watched a documentary that showed his troops captur-

ing Srebrenica on July 11, 1995, recorded by a Serbian television crew from his own TV Pale. He is shown in a room ne-
gotiating with Colonel Tom Karremans, the Dutch UN
battalion commander. Mladić stands facing the colonel, dan-
gerously near him. He is perspiring heavily. Mladić is barking
at Karremans—barking, not shouting. Because Mladić is
much shorter than the colonel, he barks even louder than
necessary. Surrounded by his heavily armed soldiers, he is
very convincing in making clear that Karremans and his 450
people are Mladić's prisoners.

In a badly lit hotel room in the village of Bratunac, Karremans repeats one gesture over and over. He lifts his left hand
to his throat and holds it there for a brief moment, as if having trouble breathing. After a couple of moments he does it
again. And again. It appears to be an involuntary, compulsive
movement, and the colonel is perhaps not even aware that
he is doing it. But he must feel something, perhaps mortal
danger. He is a tall, slim man of about fifty, dressed in a uniform, and his face is frozen with fear. Leaning back against
the wall of the hotel room, Tom Karremans touches his
throat as if to protect it from being cut.

At one point in the documentary Mladić softens his tone
a little and offers Karremans a cigarette. "Do you smoke?" he
asks. "No, I don't," Karremans says. "Oh, take it, it's not your
last one!" Mladić says laughing, recognizing the other man's
fear. The colonel has no choice but to take the cigarette. A
while later Mladić asks him if he wants to drink some beer.
Again Karremans refuses. In order not to appear impolite or

to offend the hostile Mladić, he even goes to the trouble of explaining that he doesn't think that he should drink alcohol because his soldiers are not allowed to drink. Mladić laughs wholeheartedly at him again: "You will drink it, all right!" he says. And indeed Karremans will drink. The very next moment the colonel and Mladić are clinking glasses and drinking together.

When I see Karremans standing there in front of Mladić, so frightened that he is probably thinking, this is it, this is my end, I understand that he could not have defended anybody, not even himself. It is clear that Karremans will obey Mladić, whatever he demands. Karremans is defeated, the UN troops are defeated, Srebrenica is defeated; and I read it all in the face of the Dutch commander.

The meeting of the two commanders captured on camera is an extraordinary document. Mladić deliberately humiliates the detained UN officer, who is not even an enemy but a neutral officer. "I want to help you," he says to Karremans, "although you don't deserve it, neither as a human being nor as an officer." Mladić bullies him, insults him, threatens him in front of his soldiers and the TV camera. UN neutrality means nothing to him. He does not recognize the international intervention in what he considers to be his war. Foreigners only mess things up, as he says often.

The documentary reveals him as an aggressive, narcissistic person, full of himself after having taken the Srebrenica enclave. But it also shows Mladić lying. He lies to Karremans in telling him that the Muslim population is not the aim of his action. In Potočari, he tells thousands of exhausted women and children not to be afraid, that nothing will happen to them, even though the buses that are to drive them away from their homes have already been ordered. He also lies to a Muslim representative of Srebrenica who, at the mere sight of General Mladić, is barely able to speak. Mladić tells him ". . . to all those who lay down their weapons I guarantee they will live. You have my word as a man and a general."

This habit of lying practiced by many Serbian politicians and army men caused much confusion at the beginning of the war. Everybody lied: Milošević, Karadžić, and Mladić. For a long time foreign negotiators took their promises at face value, only to realize later that they had been lied to. Obviously they didn't have the same idea of honesty. According to the Serbian understanding of the ethics of this war, lies were permitted in order to fool the enemy, to outsmart him. Indeed, it would be foolish to be truthful. Of course Mladić did not intend to imprison Muslim soldiers who laid down their arms. In Srebrenica, Mladić did not take prisoners. After he gave his officer's word of honor that the prisoners would live, it was only a matter of hours before the executions began. The bloodbath that followed after July 12 was the biggest massacre in Europe after World War II, a massacre that ended the lives of 7,475 Muslim men from Srebrenica.

As a commander, Mladić had charisma, and he knew it. Indeed, he was the most charismatic leader of them all. With Serbs, just being a soldier carries a certain prestige. As a soldier, he was ascetic, disciplined, unafraid of the front line, uncorrupted, not somebody eager to enrich himself on the black market. He gathered Serbian peasants in Bosnia and made a proper army out of them. There are many anecdotes about him as a commander; they all tell essentially the same story: he was not afraid of the enemy. Brutal and arrogant, convinced of his own military genius, he respected no one: not the international representatives, not foreign troop commanders, not the press. Serbs from Republika Srpska, on the other hand, saw in him a father figure, somebody who protected and sheltered them. At the height of his career in 1995, Mladić was the most popular person in Republika Srpska, more popular than the president Radovan Karadžić. At the same time he was the most hated and feared man in the Balkans, rivaling only Slobodan Milošević himself.

The Serbian press often compared Mladić to Prince Lazar Hrebljanović, the man who led the Serbian forces in the battle against the Turks at Kosovo Polje in 1389. The day before the battle, the prophet Elijah flew from Jerusalem and appeared to Prince Lazar in the form of a gray falcon, offering him a choice: he could either win the battle and conquer a terrestrial kingdom or lose the battle and gain a place in heaven for himself and his people. Prince Lazar did not hesitate. He chose to sacrifice his troops. And ever since that day when that battle was lost—June 28, Saint Vitus Day—Serbs have considered themselves a "celestial people," a different kind of community because they chose martyrdom.

This is the most powerful Serbian myth, one that, surprisingly, is alive even today. Or, more accurately, it has been revived, as Serbs, like any other nation, revive their myths in

difficult times. And now again, after so many centuries, the
Serbs were fighting against the Turks. They were not the
same Ottoman Turks from 1389, but they were Turks nevertheless, or *balijas,* a derogatory name for the Bosnian Muslims. This time the war was fought not at Kosovo Polje but in
Bosnia. And it was lost again. Nevertheless, like the prince in
the myth of the battle at Kosovo Polje, Mladić became a celestial warrior, a mythological hero.

One could say that the history of the Serbian people is a
history of lost battles, but according to the Kosovo myth, defeat here means victory. In his first address to the nation after his defeat by NATO in 1999, Slobodan Milošević, then the
president of the country, congratulated the Serbs on their
triumph. He did it in the best tradition of the Kosovo battle,
turning military defeat on earth into a spiritual victory. Like
Prince Lazar, given a choice between history and mythology,
Milošević chose mythology. But God did not intervene in his
case and Milošević survived the NATO bombardments in
1999, an ordinary war criminal.

Interestingly enough, Milošević was never compared to
Prince Lazar. However, the general of the forces of the Republika Srpska, Ratko Mladić, was. Soldiers are better material for mythological heroes, for epic poems and martyrdom.
Milošević was merely a politician, and their popularity comes
and goes. He still must convince his people that he is a
mythological hero, that he was defending the country from
allied Western enemies, and he is trying to do it at the tribunal in The Hague. Mladić, as a soldier, has already done it. In
recent Serbian mythology, Mladić stands above Milošević.

On old Serbian icons, Prince Lazar is depicted as a thin, pale, spiritual man. There is nothing ethereal about Mladić. But he emanated power, and people were indeed impressed by that. Mladić was very much aware of his celestial fame, and he spoke as though from above: when one journalist dared to ask Mladić who paid him and to whom he paid his taxes, Mladić gave him a heroic, celestial answer: "I don't work for money. My reward is the survival of my nation. There is no money that could pay me. . . . The meaning of my life is to give to people what I could in these difficult times."

His arrogance came as much from his character as from his situation, from living not so much in the real world as in the mythological one. Even in his public speeches he could mix past and present in a single sentence. When he took Srebrenica, he said in front of a TV camera, "I give this town to the Serbian people as a gift for Saint Vitus Day. We finally took revenge on the Turks!" Some six hundred years after the battle at Kosovo Polje, General Mladić spoke about taking revenge on the Turks even though there were no longer any Turks in Bosnia. In his mythological world, he, the archangel of Serbian revenge, finally brought justice to his people when he ordered the execution of thousands of "Turks" (that is, Bosnian Muslims) in Srebrenica. In his mind, historical justice was finally done.

• • •

That evening, as the Mladić family sat together around their table, there were no hints or premonitions of what was going to happen only twenty-four hours later. Ana had a headache that had been bothering her for some time, ever since she came back from an excursion with her fellow students to Moscow. She was one of the best students of medicine at the University of Belgrade and almost at the end of her studies. The trip to Moscow was one traditionally taken by students in their last year. The general was not pleased with the idea, but mother and daughter together somehow persuaded him to allow Ana to go, so off she went.

When she returned, she was another person. She started to complain about severe headaches and said she could not concentrate on her upcoming exam. The often-mentioned reason for her suicide is that she was finally confronted with the truth about the war. At some point perhaps she read something in the news, perhaps about what happened in Sarajevo. And Ana for the first time realized her father's role in the killings in Bosnia.

If it is true that this was why Ana Mladić committed suicide, I think I understand it. She could not confront him, could not demand an explanation or urge him to deny what she had read. Their family was a traditional, patriarchal family, and Ana had been taught never to challenge her father's authority. I know what that is like: my father was an officer, too. In our world such fathers often make no distinction between their families and their soldiers; they do not talk, they issue commands. They don't expect anybody to contradict them, especially about their work. I could never confront my father; I had to leave home to escape his overwhelming authority. In such a home there is no way for a child to ask his or her father about his job, even if it is evident that his job is to order the execution of civilians. Besides, Ana was not a male; and in spite of Mladić's love for his daughter, when it came down to serious matters like war, a woman—if she was even present at such a discussion—should listen, not talk.

If she had dared that evening to say something to him, even to mention the war, he would have looked at her with his piercing blue eyes, which would turn as cold as ice. A look of disbelief, then anger. Who was she to question him, her father? A general. Nobody would dare to address him in such a tone, not even foreign diplomats or his highest commanders. My father's eyes were like that, and when he looked at me with those cold eyes I used to feel weak in my knees. It was fear. I would look to my mother for help. But if I dared to retort to my father, if he had already given me that look and raised his voice, my mother would just watch us helplessly as if paralyzed. My mother never defended me, and I can never forget that. Ana's mother would probably have done the same. Now, though my father is long dead, I still remember my helplessness in front of him and my mother's lost, submissive look.

Ana would have had to be a very strong person indeed to stand up to her father. Many times I have tried to imagine the dialogue that might have taken place. She would, if she could, ask him: Why? Why all these killings? He would answer her that she didn't understand; this was a war, and it was his job to defend his people. But what about women, children, old people? Why kill them; they were not soldiers?

Muslims were killing children and women as well, he would answer. And for the first time he would realize that Ana was no longer his little girl but a young woman with different values from her father, and this would shock him. Don't you believe me? he would ask her. No, I don't, she would say. Her response would infuriate him and he would start to shout, forgetting that he was not among his soldiers.

Or perhaps she would ask him if all that she read about him was true: did he really order the killing of thousands of civilians in Sarajevo? Mladić would deny everything, would accuse her of believing the enemy propaganda. Lying to his own daughter would come easily to him; he had lied to others so many times before. It would nevertheless frustrate him that his own daughter dared challenge him.

But imagining this conversation is wrong. Because if Ana and her father had been able to talk to each other, she wouldn't be dead now. He will never, as long as he lives—and this is also a part of his suffering—be able to understand why Ana killed herself. And the answer is in their game of Sinking Ships: of two young grown-up people sitting with their parents and playing a children's game with them rather than watching television or going out with their friends. Ana and Darko probably wanted to do something else, but they knew their father all too well, knew his whims and silly requests. It was he who demanded they play with him because it was his way to relax. They could not refuse him. He loved to have his family around him to play some innocent game, as if nothing else of importance was happening, as if there was no war going on, as if all was well as long as the four of them were sitting around the table together playing childish games.

While they played that night, Ana must have known everything. Days before she had read articles about her father. Before that, like many of her friends, she had avoided dealing with the war. She was aware that her father was a popular chief commander of the troops of the Republika Srpska, and she was proud of him; but she did not know and did not want to know that his job was ethnic cleansing. Until it became inevitable. Until it became too late to really face it and survive.

So there she sat playing, even joking that she was going to win. The general's favorite game of Sinking Ships was not innocent, of course: it is a military game. Even at his own kitchen table Mladić couldn't escape from what he was and who he was. That evening Ana again complained about her headaches. But the signal was not clear enough, because she said nothing else, nothing more. You are probably getting the flu, her mother said, touching her forehead lightly. Her father looked at her worriedly but said nothing.

No, I won't say anything to my father, Ana probably thought. It would be impossible, she had already gone over it many times. She didn't have the strength to destroy this family idyll. She couldn't do that, not in front of her mother and her little brother. Her mother would become pale and speechless. Her brother would jump to her defense if their father started shouting or perhaps tried to hit her.

The evening before her suicide, she looked at him differently. Her father was no longer the same person to her. Her headache was real, but it was only an excuse for withdrawing. The truth was that she couldn't bear to look at him anymore.

Suddenly she felt nauseated. She looked at him, at the Butcher of Bosnia (she had read in the newspapers that this was his nickname), as if seeing him for the first time. Ana looked at her father, at his big hands, his favorite ring, his already very gray hair, and a feeling of sadness overwhelmed her, a feeling of loss. Was it possible that she was sitting across from a man accused of war crimes and saying nothing? And that this person was her father, her beloved father? Was it possible that he was so hard, so cynical, so inhuman? He smiled at her. She smiled back, a vague little smile, and made a move, sinking one of his ships. She hated herself for being so weak, so squeamish, Daddy's little girl. The headache became stronger. I have to go to bed, she said. Her mother looked at her. She sensed that something was wrong with her daughter, but just how wrong, she didn't know.

The lamp cast a circle of yellowish light on the family kitchen table. The game was over. Ana had won.

Ana had one more chance in the morning. Mladić was really worried about her and finally asked her what was the matter. She said only that she couldn't explain her behavior. He left Belgrade and went to Bosnia, sure that her strange mood would soon be over, that she was nervous and worried because of the forthcoming exam.

That next night Ana took her father's pistol, one of three he kept in their house, the special one that was given to him for being the best student in the military academy in Belgrade, the one that Mladić had told Ana that he would fire to salute the birth of his first grandson. She took that one, as if she wanted to hurt her father even more.

Away in Bosnia with his soldiers, at the moment when his daughter killed herself the general was awakened from his sleep. He felt a blow in his heart, he said later. He told his orderly that something terrible must have happened and that he should immediately call the front line. But the front line was quiet. Then the telephone rang. It was his son calling.

Mladić was convinced that she had been murdered. This to him was the only logical explanation. Ana would never kill herself. He could not conceive that his daughter, his own daughter, who played Sinking Ships with him at twenty-three, could condemn him for what he did. He could not understand it. Instead of talking, they were playing childish games. To think she had been killed was easier for him: it relieved him of all responsibility. To understand why she committed suicide would require him to admit—at least to himself—that he had indeed committed war crimes. This General Mladić could never do. Not even the death of his dear child could make him acknowledge it. It was as if he had to sacrifice his own daughter—not his soldiers and his own life, as Prince Lazar did—to become a mythological hero. If this was the price for his immortality, the gods left him alive only to make him endure the incredible pain.

This is the point where Serbian mythology meets Greek tragedy: Mladić was punished for what he did in Bosnia. He destroyed Bosnia, but finally Bosnia finished him. If Ana had been killed by a human hand, by the hand of an enemy, that would have been a human revenge. But she laid a hand on herself. The gods took revenge on Mladić. His life was like a Greek tragedy in which the gods interfere in the hero's life and punish him for his hubris while he is still alive. Mladić finally experienced the pain that he inflicted on thousands of people in Sarajevo, Srebrenica, and Goražde. But was it the same pain? Can a butcher experience the same feelings as his victims? Yes, because the pain of a parent who has lost his child is a universal one.

This loss, Mladić's biggest loss and the suffering that went with it, turned him from a mythological hero into a human being again.

After I left home, at just sixteen, my father did not speak to me for years. He was as hard as stone. He wrote me off. Why? I often wondered. Because I dared to do things on my own and not listen to him. But perhaps I would have listened to him if only he had talked to me; talked, not shouted. It is too late now. But I often dream about my father. I dream that I am standing at the top of a spiral staircase. My father is at the bottom. He is looking up at me and seems to be trying to tell me something. I see his mouth moving, but no words reach me. I wake up sobbing.

Perhaps the general, too, dreams about the lost daughter who is trying to tell him something that he doesn't hear. He wakes up in a cold sweat next to his silent wife, who deep down knows all too well who is responsible for Ana's suicide.

This is why as of March 1994 General Mladić has been serving a life sentence, even though he is a war criminal, sought by the tribunal in The Hague, who is still at large.

CHAPTER 12

The Metamorphosis of Biljana Plavšić

Not many women took part in the war, especially at the top level. Biljana Plavšić was one of the three highest-ranking officials in Republika Srpska during the war, next to Radovan Karadžić and Momčilo Krajišnik, both indicted by the tribunal. Plavšić was sentenced to eleven years in prison for crimes against humanity, violations of the laws and customs of war, and grave breaches of the Geneva Convention. She is one of the very few war criminals to have acknowledged her own responsibility.

THE ONLY woman accused of war crimes, the "iron lady" of Republika Srpska, sits calmly in the dock of the tribunal in The Hague. It is February, it is cold, and she is dressed in an elegant black suit and an olive green turtleneck pullover, a big cross hanging from a chain around her neck. From time to time she leans pensively on her hand or jumps nervously in her chair. But when Judge Richard May reads her sentence—eleven years in prison—Biljana Plavšić does not change the expression on her face. For the seventy-two-year-old, eleven years of imprisonment might be the rest of her life. Yet she looks directly into his eyes, unflinching. Composed, calm, and solemn, she maintains her poise. No one can guess what is she thinking.

Biljana Plavšić looks very good for her age. Her grayish hair is cut to shoulder length and she uses very little makeup, only some mascara for her eyelashes and discreet lipstick. Pastel or jewel-toned outfits are her usual form of dress, her trademarks. Pale green, lavender, fuchsia, and dark blue seem to be her favorite colors; a silk shirt under her jacket part of her uniform.

I must admit that under the circumstances Biljana Plavšić looks impeccable. There is one photo of her that captures this very well: it shows her visiting soldiers in the field, her cheerful pink suit standing out among camouflage uniforms, just as surely as her feminine appearance stands out among rough male faces. Nothing could have contrasted more with the uniforms than her bright-colored apparel à la Chanel, except perhaps an evening dress. She looks as if she doesn't belong there, not because she is a woman but because she is a lady.

This is how she looks in the courtroom, too: as if she doesn't belong there.

Her attitude in the court has been described as dignified. I agree; in the courtroom she does look dignified, but her dignity verges on arrogance. There is something about the way she sits there, something about her bearing, how she turns her head when she looks at the judges as if from above, as if *she* should be judging *them*. It bothers me, her air of superiority.

Biljana Plavšić irritates me until I recognize something

very familiar about her—or does she irritate me only because I recognize it? She reminds me of my mother. My
mother intimidates people just by being who she is, even today at seventy-six. And it has nothing to do with her power
or her position, because she has never had either. When I was
young, I never liked to invite my friends to our house because of my mother. She was considered cold and haughty,
even arrogant, because of the way she held herself, as if she
thought herself a queen. It now strikes me that Plavšić must
be the same type of woman. Some people seem to have an
inborn dignified or arrogant attitude (it depends on the in-
terpretation). Such people make you feel uneasy, make you
feel as if something is wrong with you: you have messy hair
or a dirty spot on your dress or you've said something stupid.
It's not that they want to make you feel that way, it's just
their way of being; and, because of it, they seem to disregard
people, often unaware that they are doing so. Some foreign
diplomats have described Plavšić as cold and unpleasant,
noting that while other Serbian politicians were warm and
forthcoming she would not even shake hands with them.

In fact, while sitting in the courtroom, Plavšić looks exactly like what she used to be before she launched herself
into high politics: a distinguished professor. More precisely,
she was an accomplished professor of biology at the University of Sarajevo who spent some time in the United States on
a Fulbright grant. It is hard to say what made her leave her
profession. Probably, as in most cases, the answer is banal:
the lust for power. But I can easily imagine what her situation looked like in 1990 just before the war in Bosnia broke

out. She was sixty years old and soon bound to retire. Ambitious and intelligent, she was not attracted by that prospect. She had no husband and no children or grandchildren to devote her time to. More importantly, she saw what kind of people entered politics. A few of them were her colleagues, academics like Nikola Koljević, a well-known expert on Shakespeare who committed suicide in 1997. But most of them were rather uncultured, half-literate men with no ambition except to profit personally from being in power. Of course she thought that she could be a better and more competent politician than they. With no family obligations and a lot of energy, she threw herself into politics. She was certainly driven by ambition, but unlike her male colleagues, she seems to have remained uncorrupted. One should not forget that when she realized how much corruption there was in her government, she started an anticorruption purge and formed a party of her own, which won the elections in 1997.

But there was a price to be paid for being the only woman among those macho Balkan politicians. A woman in such a position had to be far better than the men, and under the circumstances, for Biljana Plavšić, that meant she had to be more radical in her rhetoric. And she was.

The fact that a woman could be responsible for some of the most horrible atrocities committed in Bosnia during the war must be hard to swallow for anyone who believes—even vaguely—that if women ruled, the world would be a better place. When this woman ruled Bosnia, it was pure hell.

In the Republika Srpska, she was formally second only to the president, Radovan Karadžić. It is hard to say how much power she really had and how much she was manipulated by Slobodan Milošević and Radovan Karadžić, if she was not serving as just a form of decoration. "She had never been brought into any of the discussions, any of the decisions, and any of the meetings to deal with the critical issues of war, peace and power," said Carl Bildt, the former international high representative in Bosnia, when testifying at her trial. But even if she had little power, she knew what was going on, and in court she did not deny it.

Because she is a woman, I found it difficult to follow Biljana Plavšić over the decade of her political career. It was painful to listen to her hard-core nationalist speeches and her metaphors borrowed from biology, as when she tried to explain that Muslims in Bosnia were a "genetic mistake on the Serbian body" and that to eliminate them was a "natural phenomenon," not a war crime. Even Slobodan Milošević considered her too radical, deeming her qualified for the madhouse. It was terrible to think that she, as one of the formal heads of the secret police of the Republika Srpska as well as one of the military commanders, must have been aware of the starvation, torture, and killing of Muslim prisoners in the most terrible concentration camps of Omarska, Keraterm, and Manjača. Another photo of her from the war shows her kissing the notorious criminal Željko Ražnatović Arkan just hours after his Serbian paramilitary troops entered Bijeljina and killed forty-eight people. The corpses were still lying in the streets—indeed, she had to step over one body in order to throw her arms around Arkan's neck, kiss him, and congratulate him on the successful elimination of the genetic mistake.

When she heard that she was indicted, she immediately surrendered herself to the tribunal in January 2001, firmly believing that she had fulfilled her duty in defending her people and therefore could not be guilty of genocide, crimes against humanity, violations of the laws and customs of war, and breaches of the Geneva Convention, with which she was charged by the International Criminal Tribunal for the former Yugoslavia. Indeed, her first statement in front of the tribunal was the usual not guilty plea.

After spending a short period of time in prison, she was released on bail. The real shock came from a video-link declaration in October 2002 when Plavšić changed her original statement and confessed her guilt. This caused consternation among many Serbs: what was the matter with this woman? What did she hope to achieve? Speculations were running high. Perhaps she was hoping for a reduced sentence in exchange for testifying against Milošević? After all, she was known as a cool and calculating person, and such deals with the prosecutors and the court itself were part of juridical practice and could not be ruled out.

But Biljana Plavšić surprised us all. When she was given the chance to speak at the tribunal in December of the same year, she cut the figure of a person altogether different from what we had seen before. So different, in fact, that she was unrecognizable. In her short address she was sincere, modest, moving, and full of remorse.

It is nothing less than a miracle that once on trial, Biljana Plavšić did not say, I did not know; did not say, I was only doing my job, and did not try to evoke sympathy because she was the only woman in that Balkan world of male politicians. She had by now changed her plea to guilty of crimes against humanity (in response, the prosecution dropped the rest of the charges against her). "I am convinced and I accept that several thousand innocent people were victims of organized and systematic actions to remove Muslims and Croats from a territory that Serbs consider to be theirs," she said to the court. That statement is unprecedented.

To the question that she herself posed—how was it possible that Serbs could commit war crimes?—her answer was: blinding fear, which led to the obsessive determination never to become victims again, as the Serbs had been during the Second World War, when civil war raged between them and Croats. "In this obsession not to become victims ever again, we allowed ourselves to become perpetrators," she admitted. However, she did not bother to note that this latent fear dating back to the Second World War had been whipped up by the media and, years before any fighting broke out, prepared the collective mind-set to allow the crimes that followed.

Confronted with the accusation of the inhuman treatment of non-Serbs, she confirmed that she had heard about it but did not check to see if it was true because at that time she believed that her people could not be capable of such deeds. She conceded that the notion of self-defense is no excuse for war crimes, and she now accepted her full responsibility. Her words acknowledging guilt are important also because she is the first—and so far the only—political or military leader at the International Tribunal to accept responsibility.

In her short plea, Plavšić also found a way to appeal to the judges to seek justice for the victims and for all three sides in the war. "I can only do what is in my power and hope that it will be of some use—to understand the truth, to say it, and to accept responsibility. This, I hope, will help Muslim, Croat, and Serbian innocent victims not to be dominated by bitterness that often turns into hatred, which, at the end, leads to self-destruction." Her aim was not a milder sentence because, as she later put it, any sentence of more than ten years in her case might be the rest of her life. But she refused to cooperate with the tribunal by appearing as a prosecution witness in other trials, especially that of Milošević.

Her speech must be seen as more than an act of personal courage. It is historic for the simple reason that after her admission that Serbs were perpetrators, nobody can deny it any longer, not when it comes from someone at such a high level, from the top brass. Her words might therefore have serious consequences for the process of sobering up the vast majority of Serbs who have not even yet started to articulate their responsibility for the war. This, at least, was the hope at the ICTY in The Hague. But back in the Republika Srpska and in Serbia, the first reaction to her guilty plea was unexpected: her plea was condemned, and she was proclaimed a traitor. It will take more than her trial to force the Serbs to deal with their role in the war in Bosnia.

Biljana Plavšić nevertheless proved herself a person of some moral stamina and strength, prepared to accept the consequences of her deeds. Facing her judges, she demonstrated a remarkable readiness to accept her punishment. Her behavior is admirable, I must admit.

As she used to be the most radical person in the government of Republika Srpska, so she is now the most radical one in remorse. During the war perhaps she had to be more militant than the men surrounding her in order to be considered their equal. Of course, the interesting question is, what made her change her mind now?

Plavšić herself has given us no answers. However, there are some hints. In her address, Biljana Plavšić mentioned the loss of honor of the Serbian people because of the war crimes they committed. And then she went on to talk about the role that the saint Sava occupies in Serbian history. The Serbian leadership had departed from the saint's road of respect, nobility, and honor, she said. But why, one asks, would she mention a medieval saint as an example? The answer may be contained in what is most visible when one takes a closer look at her in the courtroom: the cross hanging ostentatiously from her neck for everybody to see. There is no doubt that it is a statement. Can it be that her religious belief made her change her mind? Or was it something completely different that made her confess her guilt: her rational scientist's mind? Faced with unquestionable proof in the court, she changed her mind, as every true scientist would do, in spite of ideology. Her rationality, it seems to me, can be proved by the fact that she really contributed to the realization of the

Dayton Agreement in 1995, that she confronted the rampant corruption, and that she cooperated with international organizations afterward.

Whatever it was that brought about her moral metamorphosis, Biljana Plavšić not only set a positive example; she also delivered a lecture on patriotism to her male colleagues, to war criminals like Radovan Karadžić and Ratko Mladić, and to Croatian "heroes" like Ante Gotovina, hiding somewhere in Herzegovina. While he hides like a coward, she, a woman, had the courage to admit her own personal guilt, thereby trying to rid her people of the prejudice that every Serb must be guilty just by definition.

This must be a hard, even humiliating, lesson for men to take from a woman in a society as patriarchal as our Balkan one. Men like Karadžić, Mladić, and Gotovina will not forgive her for having exposed them as even more miserable figures than they already were.

CHAPTER 13

Why We Need Monsters

"WHY ARE you writing about war criminals?" a friend asked me when I told her that I would be going to The Hague for five months to follow trials at the International Criminal Tribunal for the former Yugoslavia. I understood her question; she meant: haven't you had enough of that?

Yes, I had. When I finished my last novel *S.*—my second book about the war in the Balkans—I was very, very tired of the war. Year after year for ten years, I had tried to understand and explain to others the reason for the war, how it came about and how it unmistakably changed people around me and me as well. I wanted to write about something else for a change. But my thoughts kept coming back to the war. I simply could not put it behind me yet; there were too many questions, too many loose ends. The 1991–1995 war was something that I, like many others, could not have imagined. I never thought it possible in Yugoslavia, and I had to come to terms with it in some way. Writing was one way. But writing two war books was not enough. After all, that war changed my life. Confronted with nationalism, my daughter left Croatia in 1991 to live abroad. I lost the country of my birth and a lot of my friends. My world shrank to an almost homogenous Croatia. Excommunicated from its public life, I spent more and more time abroad, until finally I found myself living in Sweden, now my second homeland.

Nevertheless, the war would not leave me alone. A few years ago I gave a reading in Berlin from my novel *S.*, which was about mass rapes of Muslim women in Bosnia. As usual, after the reading there was a discussion with the audience. A young man stood up and asked me if I now would consider writing a book from the perspective of a perpetrator. "No, I will not!" I answered, almost too eagerly, as if doing so would be a crime. True, my books about the war were written from the perspective of the victims. The horror of the war could truly be described only from their position, I thought. The world already knew enough about the perpetrators. How many articles had been written about Slobodan Milošević? Thousands upon thousands. In time, thanks to the media, Slobodan Milošević, Radovan Karadžić, and Ratko Mladić had practically become celebrities; whatever their crimes had been was no longer remembered or even important. If one attempts to write from the viewpoint of the perpetrators, to try to understand such people, how close can one come to justifying their acts? Can we, in fact, understand war criminals? More important, why should we even try? These were the questions that went through my mind as I thought about how ominous it was that this subject was raised in, of all places, Germany.

I did not realize at the time that in response to that young German reader's inquiry, I had reacted in a typically self-defensive way, in exactly the same way as when, two years later, other people would react when I told them that I was writing about the perpetrators, that is, war criminals. Why are you interested in them? They are monsters, they'd say.

It is easy to understand such reactions. War criminals have committed indescribable acts, and nobody wants to be connected to them in any way. But this doesn't bring us closer to the essential question: how were such crimes possible? If we believe their perpetrators are monsters, it is because we wish to create as great a distance as possible between us and them, to exclude them from humanity altogether. We even go so far as to say that their crimes were inhuman, as if evil (as well as good) were not a part of human nature. At the bottom of such reasoning there is a syllogism: ordinary people could not have done what these monsters did; we are ordinary people, therefore we cannot commit such crimes.

But once you get closer to the real people who committed those crimes, you see that the syllogism doesn't really work.

In 1993 I followed the trial of Borislav Herak, a Serb from Bosnia who was sentenced to death (later reduced to life imprisonment) by a court in Sarajevo for sixteen rapes and the murder of 32 civilians (12 of them raped women) and for his participation in the killing of 220 Muslims. My biggest disappointment was finding that this was a man who looked like any other man: a neighbor, a relative, or even a friend. I looked almost desperately for a trace of madness in his eyes, for any evidence that he was different—in short, that he was a monster. And I was not the only person looking for such signs in war criminals. Many have done the same.

Does some personality flaw—or a specific type of character—cause human cruelty? Is there in every community a certain percentage of people who have the pathology to commit the worst crimes if given the chance? Or do they commit crimes only under social and psychological pressure? These questions are not new. There is a whole library of competently written books about this issue, many of which appeared just after World War II (for example, by Raul Hilberg, Theodor Adorno, Zygmunt Bauman, John Steiner, and Ervin Staub). As we are newly confronted with such cases, the questions about the nature of their behavior are as disturbing now as ever.

Surely there are cases bordering on the pathological (Goran Jelisić being one), but the quantity and brutality of crimes committed (mass rapes in Bosnia, for example) suggest that either the number of sick people is rather large or something else is at work. In his book *Ordinary Men,* the American historian Christopher Browning analyzes the case of the 101st Reserve Battalion and the final solution in Poland. He concludes that those German men who were sent first to kill thousands of Polish Jews were not specially chosen or in any way different from other Germans. On the contrary, the battalion was composed of people from all walks of life and in that way was truly representative of ordinary men.

An unemployed twenty-two-year-old, Borislav Herak was not interested in politics nor did he personally hate Muslims. But when he was given a chance to kill them on some apparently legitimate grounds and, in addition, to enrich himself by looting his victims, he did not think twice. What was frightening about watching Herak on trial was realizing that he was neither a nationalist nor a madman.

But if there was something in his character that made him behave pathologically (and I don't deny that there may be such cases), there is no more reason for us to occupy ourselves with Herak and others like him than to study exotic insects in the Amazon. Such cases tell us only that there are people who are mad or sick and whose behavior has no relevance for ordinary people who are not similarly afflicted.

The more I have occupied myself with the individual cases of war criminals, the less I believe them to be monsters. What if they *are* ordinary people, just like us, who found themselves in particular circumstances and made wrong moral decisions? What might this tell us about *ourselves*?

You sit in a courtroom watching a defendant day after day and at first you wonder, as Primo Levi did, "if this is a man." No, this is not a man, it is all too easy to answer, but as the days pass you find the criminals become increasingly human. Soon you feel that you know them intimately. You watch their faces, ugly or pleasant, their small habits of yawning, taking notes, scratching their heads, cleaning their nails, and you have to ask yourself: what if this *is* a man? The more you know them, the more you wonder how they could have committed such crimes, these waiters and taxi drivers, teachers and peasants in front of you. And the more you realize that war criminals might be ordinary people, the more afraid you become. Of course, this is because the consequences are more serious than if they were monsters. If ordinary people committed war crimes, it means that any of us can commit them. Now you understand why it is so easy and comfortable to accept that war criminals are monsters, rather than to agree with Ervin Staub that "evil that arises out of ordinary thinking and is committed by ordinary people is the norm, not the exception."

Indeed, it seems to me that brutality in war is more the norm than the exception, and more to do with circumstances than with character. But if this is really the case, none of us can be sure how we would behave in those particular circumstances. In short, there are no guarantees, as numerous psychological tests have proved. For example, in his famous 1971 Stanford Prison simulation experiment in inducing pain on command, Philip Zimbardo found that in only a few days the "guards" became so sadistic that he had to abandon the experiment. "How could intelligent, mentally healthy, 'ordinary' men become perpetrators of evil so quickly?" he asked. As frightening as this idea is, it is precisely the reason we should learn more about extraordinary situations and ordinary people's reactions to them. This is why we need to learn more about perpetrators and how they came to be. The young German reader was right. Only if we understand that most perpetrators are people like us can we see that we too might one day be in danger of succumbing to the same kind of pressure.

· · ·

Yet a question remains: what must happen to make that ordinary man see an enemy in a colleague or a neighbor? How is it possible for hatred, humiliation, brutality, and even murder to become legitimate behavior? One policeman

from the 101st Reserve Battalion admitted that to his unit
Jews were not human beings. What political, social, and psychological processes in a society make such thinking possible? What makes mass hatred possible, and what makes
possible the ethnic cleansing that it can engender?

Perhaps it is far-fetched to compare Nazi Germany with
any part of the former Yugoslavia. But one element makes
such a comparison feasible, and that is the construction of
the other as the object of hatred. To begin with, it is important to identify that object and give compelling reasons for
hatred. The reasons do not have to be rational or even necessarily true. The most important thing is that they are convincing, because this makes them acceptable to people. Such
explanations are usually based on myths (the myth of Serbs
as a celestial people, for example, or the myth about the
Croatians' thousand-year-old dream of having their own
state) and prejudices (Serbs are primitive, Croats are Nazis,
Muslims are stupid). And it helps if these myths and prejudices are rooted in reality, either in the history of earlier wars
or in cultural and religious differences.

As we still see in many parts of the world, the object of
hatred can also be people belonging to another tribe (Hutu,
Tutsi) or a different race. The task of propaganda is to shape
this difference so that it creates a feeling that there is a threat
from the other side and strengthens the urge for homogenization. Most important is the method of introducing hatred: it is most effective if people get used to it slowly, step by
step, until they have absorbed it into their daily life.

In light of the "evidence" of differences, often in the form of detailed descriptions of pressures and suffering in the mass media, either real or invented, in time those others are stripped of all their individual characteristics. They are no longer acquaintances or professionals with particular names, habits, appearances, and characters; instead they are members of the enemy group. When a person is reduced to an abstraction in such a way, one is free to hate him because the moral obstacle has already been abolished. If it has been "proved" that our enemies are no longer human beings, we are no longer obliged to treat them as such. It doesn't count at all that by doing so we reduce ourselves to an abstract category as well, that we are no longer individuals because in the eyes of the enemy we are the others, too.

The beginning of the war in the former Yugoslavia did not differ from what Victor Klemperer wrote in *I Shall Bear Witness,* his diary from 1933 to 1941, when he described how, little by little, anti-Semitism became a normal way of thinking and behaving in Germany at that time. This perception also comes slowly to the victim: Klemperer, himself a Jew, did not want to see it and brushed it aside for years.

As in Germany, in Croatia you first stopped greeting a person of the other nationality, perhaps only because you were afraid that others would see you acknowledging him. Unbelievable as it is, this seemingly insignificant concession, this small act of adaptation to a new reality of the total national homogenization, set you on a dangerous road. Turning your face aside in fact created the opportunity for someone else to commit war crimes in the name of the very same principles of isolation and elimination of the others.

Most people in Croatia, Serbia, and Bosnia adjusted to a mixture of state propaganda, opportunism, fear, and indifference that created a norm of behavior without being properly aware of the consequences. There were very few people who were able to resist the general atmosphere of the normality of hatred. Of course, there is a difference between a person who does not greet a Serb or a Muslim neighbor and a man who kills him, just as there is a difference between a government that does not issue documents to Serbs and one that orders the wearing of yellow stars. But turning your head away or remaining silent in the face of injustice and crime means collaborating with a politics whose program is death and destruction. And whether it is willing or unwilling collaboration doesn't really matter, because the result is the same.

More than a decade after the beginning of the war in the Balkans, it is essential that we understand that it is *we,* ordinary people and not some madmen, who made it possible. *We* were the ones who one day stopped greeting our neighbors of a different nationality, an act that the next day made possible the opening of concentration camps. We did it to one another. Maybe this is a good reason for considering whether it is too easy to put a hundred men on trial in The Hague. What about the others who embraced the ideology that led to the deaths of two hundred thousand people? Perhaps they did not believe in it, but they certainly did not protest against it. If it is true that there is no collective guilt, can there be collective innocence?

Often in Croatia one heard it said that the tribunal was trying not merely a few war criminals but the defensive "war for the homeland" and the whole Croatian nation as well. In other words, guilt is not individualized. We are still prisoners of collectivism. Guilt needs individualization, which is exactly what the tribunal stands for. A whole nation, Croatian or other, could not be held *guilty* of war crimes. But the whole nation could indeed be held *responsible* for war crimes, both politically and morally. The people in Serbia twice elected Slobodan Milošević president of Serbia and once president of Yugoslavia. Croats elected Franjo Tudjman president on two occasions. To our knowledge these were reasonably free elections. If Germans were responsible for supporting Hitler, why should not Serbs be responsible for supporting Milošević and Croats for supporting Tudjman? Neither of them could have survived in power without the support of the people.

In voting for Milošević or Tudjman, people voted for the politics of ethnic cleansing. Could they claim, like the Germans, that they did not know? Both Croatia and Serbia are too small to use that as an argument. In the five years of war, too many people were directly involved in the ethnic cleansing to be able to claim seriously that they did not know. They *did* know, and they went along with it, or at least they did not care about it. This is the main reason they don't like to talk about war crimes or about the war in general, except for the notion of the heroic defensive war. It is not pleasant to learn that you were a collaborator. But it is necessary to learn that you had a choice—and that you made the wrong one. In some way, not only the war criminals but also the people who made them possible should be held responsible for their wrong choices.

The trials of war criminals are important not only because of those killed. They are important also because of the living. In the end, what matters in regard to war criminals and why we should bother to take a closer look at them is one single important question: what would *I* do in their situation? The unpleasant truth is that there is no clear answer.

Epilogue: Brotherhood and Unity

I T IS a day like any other in the Scheveningen detention unit in The Hague. While Goran Jelisić and Tihomir Blaškić walk in the courtyard, Rahim Ademi cooks lunch. His wife, who recently visited him, brought him some food from Croatia: Dalmatian prosciutto, olive oil, and fresh fish from the Adriatic Sea. The fish from the North Sea tastes different: they all agree about that. It is fat and has no taste, especially when it is boiled and served with a thick sauce, as is the custom here in the Netherlands. Could it be that there is too little salt in the North Sea?

But now, thanks to Ademi, the whole floor smells enticingly of today's meal, which is *brodetto,* a kind of fish stew. Ademi is the best cook of the twelve who live on this floor. Earlier it was another Croat, Dario Kordić, who often tended to their meals, but since Ademi came, he has practically taken over. He can make a most delicious beef Stroganoff and Viennese schnitzel, not to mention scampi in tomato sauce or calamari stuffed with garlic, a lot of parsley, bread crumbs, and the finely chopped tentacles of the squid. Everybody agrees that his lamb chops, rubbed with rosemary, thyme, and sage, are excellent. Even his ordinary chicken soup tastes better than anything they get from the common kitchen in their detention unit.

The food that they get in the Scheveningen penitentiary is, of course, something different: pale, meager, lacking any particular flavor or smell. More like what you would get in a hospital, although most of these men are reasonably healthy; and when they say "hospital" they mean one of those ragged hospitals in the country they come from. They crave the food they are used to: a good beef soup with handmade thinly cut noodles, a pita with young cheese or a loaf of crusty warm bread, roasted meat, *sarma,* and the famous *čevapčići* or *ražnjići.* (And a bottle of good Dalmatian wine to go with it—but this they don't get. No alcohol is permitted.)

Of course, nobody here minds if the meal is Bosnian or Serbian or Croatian; they are not nationalists when it comes to good food. They are just happy any time they get freshly made, tasty meals. Fortunately they can order food to be brought in from the outside. So every Monday a list is made, carefully, to accommodate everyone's wishes and tastes. If there is a holiday, a birthday, or some other occasion to celebrate, they can order a whole lamb or piglet and roast it, just as they would do back home. And they eat it together, enjoying every morsel, as they did when the detention unit's management decided to hold a holiday party for all of them in an effort to unite them even more. (It was just like during the days of communism, when instead of Christmas it was the New Year that was celebrated in Scheveningen.) The official celebration was on December 19, and celebrations of the Catholic and Orthodox Christmases and the Muslim holidays were allowed, too. The detainees roasted a whole piglet. The atmosphere was, in the words of Timothy McFadden, an Irish army officer and the director of the Scheveningen detention unit (he doesn't like it being called a prison, rightly so, since it is a separate unit within the Scheveningen prison), "very pleasant, very jolly . . . lots of salads and cooked meats and bread and what do you call it . . . baklava? . . . and plenty of music playing, that typically Yugoslavian or Balkan music. Well, I don't know which is the correct way to say it now."

In the common room Sefer Halilović is reading newspapers from Bosnia that just arrived. They all follow only what is happening back home, even if they aren't sure if ever they will return there. After Halilović has finished, Blaškić, Naletilić, Kvočka, and the others will read the same newspapers. They all read the very same newspapers regardless of which part of the former Yugoslavia they happen to come from. Language is the other thing besides food that unites them all. Like refugees scattered across continents, they usually do not specify; they call it "our language" or nothing at all. No name is needed. Of course they each have their own language, but why should they complicate life even further by naming them as long as they understand one another without doing so? The fact is that it makes no difference if they speak Serbian, Croatian, or Bosnian; they all understand one another perfectly. And where language is concerned, these men show no sign of nationalism. Except in the courtroom, sometimes. But that is more for the records:

for example, during his trial Dario Kordić complained that the translation was not in Croatian but in Serbian. He did not say that he did not understand it, only that it was not his language. Blagoje Simić remarked that he recognized some Croatian words in the simultaneous translation into Serbian. But these instances were exceptions.

Some of the men work out in the gym—a very popular place among detainees—while the others are in the tribunal. Slobodan Milošević works in his office. He has an extra cell at his disposal because he officially has no lawyer and is handling his own defense. (Unofficially he is helped by a whole crew of lawyers working for him in Belgrade.) After lunch he will most likely join other detainees from his floor—Paško Ljubičić, and Dragoljub Prćac among them—in the common room and perhaps play gin rummy with them if he is not too tired; lately, one can see that the trial is wearing on him. When Milošević was brought in, the management of Scheveningen feared that the other detainees would react aggressively toward him and therefore kept him in isolation. Indeed, some days after his arrival, Goran Jelisić attacked Milošević with his fists (of course, the two could not be kept on the same floor afterward). But Milošević's isolation did not last long, as it was soon clear that, except for Jelisić, the others accepted him as one of them. Soon he was sharing meals and newspapers with the rest of the detainees and like them spending his free time in the common room. That is, when he was not reading: Slobodan Milošević is an ardent reader. He also likes taking a stroll in the courtyard. The prison in Scheveningen is on the waterfront, and he can hear the seagulls and breathe the salty air while watching clouds chased by the wind across the sky, big golden clouds, as in Vermeer's paintings of Delft. Timothy McFadden says that by now Milošević is no less than a model prisoner. He is cordial, speaks with everyone, including the guards, doesn't seem to care about where a person comes from, and helps other inmates learn English. And he praises Dragoljub Prćac when he is in charge of the kitchen, saying that he has never eaten so well before in his life.

But some of the old prestige is still attached to Milošević: curiously enough, Ademi addresses him as Mr. President, although Milošević is no longer the president of Serbia and even less of a president to someone like the Albanian Ademi, who is a Croatian citizen.

Sitting next to Halilović are Miroslav Kvočka and Hazim Delić, playing cards. If they want to, they can visit the library, which has some six hundred books, most of them in "their" language. Or take a course in English or painting. Detainee Duško Tadić has spent quite some time painting. There are a piano and a guitar in the common room for anyone who likes to play music. Doctors and psychologists are at their service when needed; even a massage can be ordered. One of the most important privileges they enjoy is that they are allowed to smoke, both outside their rooms and in the common space as well. For the detainees, this is a blessing.

The day is gray, as it so often is in this part of Europe. A gentle rain is falling. Some of the younger men have gone out to the playground to play handball. They are not nationalists when it comes to sports; they all play together. One of them is the Bosnian Croat Mladen Naletilić Tuta, who is well over fifty. Before his extradition from Croatia, he was considered too ill to be put on a plane to The Hague. But he was put on one nevertheless, and once he was here in the Scheveningen detention unit, his health miraculously improved. It seems that Scheveningen is beneficial to health, almost like a spa. Here the detainees can spend the whole day out of their rooms, but may prefer to stay in, to take a nap or read; the rooms are clean and big enough for their comfort. Each is equipped with a shower, a writing desk, a radio, and a TV set. According to Tuta, compared with a prison in Zagreb, their quarters in Scheveningen are like rooms in a three-star hotel. The Dutch even call the prison the Orange Hotel—*Het Oranje Hotel*—not, however, because of the luxurious conditions but because it is the building in which Dutch Resistance fighters were imprisoned by the Nazis in World War II. More than fifty years later it is not heroes but suspected war criminals from the Balkans who are living in this building.

Almost as if they really were on vacation in a beach hotel, the men are generally, with very rare exceptions, pleasant to each other. They do not quarrel or make problems, says McFadden. Given that in addition to belonging to different nationalities, they are also of different backgrounds and professions—former police officers, military men, teachers, politicians, taxi drivers, waiters, and car mechanics—their harmony is an achievement. They comply with the house rules, and some are models of respect for law and order. McFadden himself is very protective of his detainees (not "pris-

oners," of course) and makes sure that they all have what
they need. Visitors may come any day; if they wish, they can
stay all day. They do need his approval to do so, but in a normal prison a visitor may not come more than once a month.
They also get a kind of pocket money, two dollars a day; and
for washing corridors and doing laundry, they can earn five
dollars a day, although there are not many candidates for
that extra money. And they get a twenty-five-dollar telephone card each month. Perhaps the biggest sensation is the
"love room," in fact, two rooms, where the detainees can receive their wives and be together with them. Thanks to this
facility, children have already been fathered by Zoran Žigić
and Tihomir Blaškić.

Why do the detainees at the Scheveningen unit enjoy
such extraordinary privileges? McFadden has a simple explanation: according to the law, these men are not guilty until
it has been proved in court that they are, and therefore they
and their families should suffer as little as possible. This is the
reason, he says, that he hasn't even read the indictments
against them, so he can avoid being prejudiced. To him, they
are not war criminals but ordinary people. However, McFadden's concern for the detainees, their rights, and their life in
comparative luxury—Scheveningen is certainly the most
comfortable detention unit in Europe—is in such dispro-
portion to the crimes they are suspected of having committed that it seems almost absurd, at least in the eyes of their
victims. And it is hardly any consolation to the victims that
the detainees won't enjoy similar privileges if they are actually sentenced and have to leave for other prisons in coun-

tries that have agreed with the United Nations to take them on, countries like Germany, Norway, and Finland.

Another thing that unites these men, besides food, language, and sports, is that they are accused of having committed the worst war crimes in Europe since 1945. One would think that since they were at war with each other and might still be deadly enemies, it would be logical to place them on different floors according to their nationalities. But here Serbs and Croats and Bosnians, who for years fought each other, live happily together. And although each of them continues to stick to the political opinions that brought him to Scheveningen, they obviously have reached a compromise that enables them to live together, something that people back home can only dream about. "When I came here, the first man who greeted me was Esad Landjo, a Muslim," said Goran Jelisić, a Serb who specialized in executing Muslim prisoners from close range. "He helped me. He told me about the rules and what was waiting for me in the court." Back home Esad Landjo specialized in torturing Serbian prisoners.

The detainees not only help each other, they act together as well. When Milan Kovačević died and Slavko Dokmanović killed himself, they sent condolences to the families and flowers to the funerals. They also signed a petition that was sent to the president of the tribunal, asking for an improvement of the conditions in the detention center, and they wrote an open letter to the media denying gossip that they were suffering from depression.

It is almost touching to see how much togetherness these

men are capable of, how much solidarity there is among them, as if the air in Scheveningen could produce miracles not only for their physical well-being but also for their souls. It is as if once the electronic door of the prison closed behind them, they turned into different men. Suddenly there is no more of the nationalism that destroyed a whole country and took a quarter of a million lives.

How is it possible? Simo Zarić, accused of persecuting people of different—that is, Muslim and Croatian—origins (still, by all accounts Zarić is small fry), is convinced that the spirit of unity among the detainees is very much what it used to be like in the old Yugoslav National Army. "One has to adjust and survive," he said.

The Yugoslav National Army? Indeed, this strikes me as an interesting comparison. The Yugoslav National Army was considered to be the best school of brotherhood and unity in the old Yugoslavia, intended to uphold the widely propagated slogan of Tito and to keep together a country of six republics, five nations, and four religions. All in vain, it seems. Because no matter how good the school was, brothers had no problem killing each other; and of unity there is not much left.

But in Scheveningen, Tito's Yugoslavia still seems to be alive. Just how peacefully the accused war criminals of different nationalities coexist is described in a poem written by Zarić himself. There one can find lines like these:

It is not important what happened there
but how it is now, here

Describing the life in the prison, the harmony and friendship of the prisoners, Zarić ends the poem with a message to people back home to follow their example!

This poem, called "Truth About The Hague," became an informal anthem of the detainees in Scheveningen, accepted by everyone there. Goran Jelisić, who acts as a kind of spokesman for the group, told the public in the court (while appearing in Landjo's trial as a character witness) that men of different nationalities in their detention unit had achieved peace among themselves but added that they had doubts that people at home were capable of achieving the same thing. Together the detainees had come to the conclusion that "the tribunal has to contribute to the establishing of a lasting peace in Bosnia."

In this conclusion they apparently see no irony.

When night falls, the men in Scheveningen withdraw into their cozy apartments, equipped with satellite dishes, so that they can watch TV programs in their own language (a service no ordinary hotel room offers), and coffee machines, so that they can have a cup of coffee, just because they are used to it; to deprive them of this would mean denying them their rights. And before they fall asleep—with or without sleeping pills—none will give a thought to the paradox of Scheveningen: that, at the end of the day, it very much looks like Yugoslavia in miniature.

The Yugoslavia of brotherhood and unity doesn't exist any longer, except in this prison.

And the men who are most responsible for its falling apart and for the thousands upon thousands of victims of that war are today living not only in unity like brothers but in luxury. The life they lead in detention is the biggest antiwar demonstration one could imagine, except that it is being staged too late and that those nice guys playing cards, cooking, and watching TV are mocking the people back home who once took them seriously. They ridicule those who followed their orders. They make fools of those who have lost their dear ones. They make all the sacrifices meaningless.

But if the brotherhood and unity among the sworn enemies of yesterday is indeed the epilogue of this war, one wonders what was it all for? Looking at the merry boys in the Scheveningen detention unit, the answer seems clear: for nothing.

Acknowledgments

I WAS LUCKY enough to get generous support from the Hamburger Stiftung zur Förderung von Wissenschaft und Kultur and from the Olaf Palme Center in Stockholm. As a fellow of the Netherlands Institute for Advanced Study in the Humanities and Social Sciences (NIAS) in Wassenaar, I had excellent conditions for work, and I was able to pay regular visits to the tribunal in the neighboring Hague. I am especially grateful to an NIAS fellow, Willem Wagenaar, a professor of psychology at the University of Leiden, for many discussions that helped me clarify my ideas. Ann Simpson was kind enough to edit my manuscript, and I would like to express my gratitude to her, too.

Mirko Klarin and Vjera Bogati from the SENSA news agency helped me with all kinds of practical matters, and I could not have possibly written this book without their help. I also would like to thank my friend Tanja Petovar for insisting that I write this book in the first place.

Kultur Kontakt in Vienna helped me with traveling expenses, and I thank them for that.

Needless to say, this book would probably look different without the wise suggestions of my husband, Richard Swartz.